# CAUGHT
## in the
# N E T

**How to Recognize
the Signs of
Internet Addiction—
and a Winning
Strategy for Recovery**

## KIMBERLY S. YOUNG

JOHN WILEY & SONS, INC.
New York ■ Chichester ■ Weinheim ■ Brisbane ■ Singapore ■ Toronto

**Author's Note**

Names, ages, places, occupations, and other identifying information have been changed to protect the privacy and confidences of persons who consulted with, or were interviewed by, the author. And some of the cases presented have been factually altered or combined for illustrative purposes.

While this book has been written to assist those who are or may be Internet addicted, it is not intended to serve as a replacement for professional medical advice. The author and publisher specifically disclaim any and all liability arising directly or indirectly from the use or application of any information contained in this book. Where appropriate, a health care professional should be consulted regarding your situation.

*Library of Congress Cataloging-in-Publication Data:*

Young, Kimberly S.
    Caught in the net : how to recognize the signs of Internet addiction—and a winning strategy for recovery / by Kimberly S. Young.
        p.    cm.
    Includes bibliographical references and index.
    ISBN 0-471-19159-0 (cloth : alk. paper)
    1. Internet addiction.   I. Title.
RC569.5.I54Y68   1998
616.86—dc21                                          97-49070

To Jim O'Mara, my husband, soulmate, and best friend, for believing in me even when I didn't.

# About the Author

Dr. Kimberly S. Young is Assistant Professor of Psychology at the University of Pittsburgh, Bradford, and founder of the Center for On-Line Addiction, which consults to educational institutions, mental health clinics, and corporations dealing with Internet misuse.

Dr. Young is known internationally for her work on Internet addiction. Her research has been widely covered in the media, including major articles in *The New York Times, The Wall Street Journal, Newsweek,* and *U.S. News & World Report.* She has appeared on news broadcasts on the major networks and has been heard on NPR and the BBC.

Dr. Young is committed to expanding the body of knowledge about Internet use and to helping individuals seek treatment for their Internet-dependence problems. Readers can contact her by e-mail at ksy@netaddiction .com and review the Center for On-Line Addiction's Web site at http://www.netaddiction.com.

# Acknowledgments

First, and most important, I want to thank all the on-lineaholics and their families who willingly and openly came forward to share their stories with me. It is your courage that provided the foundation for this book.

My utmost gratitude to Kevin Quirk; without his writing talent and organizational skill this book would not have been possible. To Jo Ann Miller, Executive Editor at John Wiley & Sons, for her literary guidance and keen insight throughout this project. To my agent, Carol Mann, for believing in the project in its early stages and for her encouragement.

To the Chair of my division at the University of Pittsburgh at Bradford, Dr. Warren Fass, and the Vice President and Dean of Academic Affairs, Dr. Carol Baker, for granting me a course reduction to work on this book. To the computer, library, public relations, and support staff at the University of Pittsburgh at Bradford for their assistance in countless tasks, especially Linda Bredengerd, Helen Handley, Colleen James, Bill Kline, Don Lewicki, Chris Mackowski, Trisha Morris, Kim Murphey, Rosanne O'Hanesian, Jackie Streb, Mark Van Tilburg, and Cheryl Verner. To my research assistant, Robert Rodgers III, for his voluntary help with the statistical analyses of my data. To Dr. Ron Mattis, for his help in developing my Web page. To Jim Matson, for his help setting up my Web page and for showing me the ins and outs of MUDding.

To those who supported my project and proofread early drafts of my work, Dr. Walter Buell, Drew Linsalata, Lisa Lis, Dr. David Lynch, Dr. Francis Mulcahy, Dr. Mary Lou Zanich, and especially my sister, Suzie Maras, your feedback has been most appreciated. To my friends who are too many to name individually, for their sympathetic listening and constant encouragement.

I want to thank the many psychological, computer, and managerial professionals I interviewed, who served as invaluable resources for the compilation of my data for this project.

I am especially grateful to all the newspapers, magazines, and radio and TV stations that publicized news of my Internet addiction survey and made it possible for readers and listeners to contact me and participate in my research.

Special thanks goes to my loving husband, Jim, who patiently supported my long hours tied to our computer and who always helped me keep my life in perspective.

Finally, I want to thank my father, Bill Meyer, whose love and devotion gave me the initial confidence to pursue this endeavor.

# Contents

# Introduction: A Controversial New Addiction

> *The surge of modems appearing in households throughout the country is creating a society of on-line addicts.* —CNN
>
> *I used to have a RL [real life] prior to this "electronic take-over."* —INTERNET USER QUOTED IN THE NEW YORKER
>
> *The Internet is not a habit. . . . it's an indelible feature of modern life.* —NEWSWEEK

Over three years ago I received an urgent phone call from my friend Marsha, a high school English teacher in North Carolina.

"I'm ready to divorce John," Marsha announced. I was taken aback. Marsha and John had been together for five years and had what I assumed was a stable marriage. I asked her what had gone wrong: Did John have a drinking problem? Was he having an affair? Had he been abusing her? "No," she replied. "He's addicted to the Internet."

Between sobs, she filled me in on the problem. Every night, he'd come home from work at 6 P.M. and head straight for the computer. No kiss hello, no help with dinner, or the dishes, or the laundry. At 10 P.M., he'd still be on-line when she'd call him to come to bed. "Be right there," he'd say. Four or five hours later, he'd finally log off and stumble into bed.

It had gone on like this for months. She'd complain to him about feeling neglected, ignored, and confused about how he could get sucked into cyberspace for 40 or 50 hours every week. He didn't listen, and he didn't stop. Then came the credit-card bills for his on-line service, $350 or more per month. "We were trying to save our money to buy a house," she said, "and he's squandering all our savings on the Internet." So she was leaving. She didn't know what else to do.

I listened to my friend as supportively as I could, but when we hung up my mind was abuzz with questions: What could anyone be doing on the computer all that time? What would lure an ordinary person into such an obsession with the Internet? Why couldn't John stop himself, especially when he could see that his marriage was in danger? Could Internet users really become addicted?

My professional curiosity was aroused, further piqued by my long-standing interest in technological wonders. I'm a clinical psychologist, but I've known the ins and outs of computers for years. I have an undergraduate degree in business, concentrating in management information systems, and I once worked for a manufacturing firm as a computer specialist. I spend as much time browsing through *Internet Today* as I do reading the latest issue of *Psychology Today.* And like millions of people all over the world, my workday begins with a quick check of my e-mail as I sip my morning coffee.

But before that distress call from Marsha, I had regarded the rapid growth of the Internet in the early 1990s as nothing more than the technological and communications marvel it was touted to be. Sure, I could remember seeing swarms of students filling the computer labs at every hour of the day and night at the University of Rochester, when I was completing my clinical fellowship at the medical school there. A strange sight, but maybe free computer access was simply encouraging students to invest more time and energy in their research papers, I figured at the time.

I also vaguely recalled a few tongue-in-cheek remarks in the media about obsessive use of the Internet. The business magazine *Inc.* made a remark about 12-step programs for Internet addicts. CNN commented on how the surge of modems suddenly appearing in households throughout the country was "creating a society of on-line addicts."

Now I listened to such comments in a new light. Ironically, the morning after my phone call with Marsha I happened to see a *Today* show report on an Internet chat room. This group spent hours on the Internet every day debating the guilt or innocence of O. J. Simpson during the ongoing criminal trial, and the chatting cost one woman $800 a month in on-line fees. Sounds strikingly similar to the effects of gambling addiction, I mused. Was there something sinister going on in cyberspace?

It was time to find out. Drawing on the same criteria used to diagnose compulsive gambling and alcoholism, I devised a short questionnaire to pose to Internet users. I asked:

- Do you feel preoccupied with the Internet (i.e., think about previous on-line activity or anticipate next on-line session)?
- Do you feel the need to use the Internet with increasing amounts of time in order to achieve satisfaction?
- Have you repeatedly made unsuccessful efforts to control, cut back, or stop Internet use?
- Do you feel restless, moody, depressed, or irritable when attempting to cut down or stop Internet use?
- Do you stay on-line longer than originally intended?

- Have you jeopardized or risked the loss of a significant relationship, job, educational, or career opportunity because of the Internet?
- Have you lied to family members, a therapist, or others to conceal the extent of your involvement with the Internet?
- Do you use the Internet as a way of escaping from problems or of relieving a distressed mood (e.g., feelings of helplessness, guilt, anxiety, depression)?

I posted the questionnaire on that November 1994 day on several Usenet groups—virtual discussion places where Internet users can send and receive messages on specific topic areas. I expected a handful of responses, and none as dramatic as Marsha's story. But the next day my e-mail was stuffed with more than 40 responses from Internet users from Vermont to Oregon, as well as messages from Canada and overseas transmissions from England, Germany, and Hungary!

Yes, my respondents wrote, they were addicted to the Internet. They stayed on-line for 6, 8, even 10 or more hours at a time, day after day, despite the problems this habit was causing in their families, their relationships, their work life, and their school work. They felt anxious and irritable when off-line and craved their next date with the Internet. And despite Internet-triggered divorces, lost jobs, or poor grades, they couldn't stop or even control their on-line usage.

Clearly the information superhighway had a few bumps in the road. Before drawing any major conclusions, however, I knew I needed more data, so I expanded the survey. I asked just how much time Internet users spent on-line for personal use (nonacademic or non-job-related purposes), what hooked them, exactly what problems their obsession triggered, what kind of treatment they had sought, if any, and whether they had a history of other addictions or psychological problems. When I concluded the survey, I had received 496 responses from Internet users. After evaluating their answers, I categorized 396 (80 percent) of these respondents as Internet addicts! From exploring the World Wide Web and reading up-to-the-minute news items and stock market trends, to participating in socially interactive chat rooms and games, Internet users admitted that they were investing more and more time on-line at greater and greater cost to their real lives.

Moving beyond this initial survey, conducted mostly through on-line exchanges of questions and answers, I followed up with more thorough telephone and in-person interviews. The more I talked to Internet addicts, the more convinced I became that this problem was real—and likely to escalate rapidly. With the Internet generally expected to reach 75 to 80 percent of the U.S. population in the next several years, and penetrating other countries just as rapidly, I realized I had tapped into a potential epidemic.

The media soon learned of my study. News stories about Internet addiction surfaced in *The New York Times*, *The Wall Street Journal*, *USA Today*, *The New York Post*, and *The London Times*. I was interviewed about this phenomenon on *Inside Edition*, *Hard Copy*, CNBC, and programs on Swedish and Japanese television. At the 1996 American Psychological Association convention in Toronto, my research paper "Internet Addiction: The Emergence of a New Clinical Disorder" was the first on the subject of Internet addiction approved for presentation. As I set up my materials, I glanced over at the badges of the journalists who began to swarm around me: Associated Press, *Los Angeles Times*, *Washington Post*. Microphones were thrust in my face and photographers snapped pictures. A professional presentation had turned into an impromptu press conference.

I had hit a nerve. In our culture's eager embracing of the Internet as the information and communications tool of the future, we had been ignoring the dark side of cyberspace. My study of Internet addicts had brought the issue to light, and since then the network of obsessive Internet users and concerned families eager to address the problem has continued to expand. I've been contacted by more than a thousand people from all over the world who share a common distress and express gratitude for having a sounding board for it.

"I can't tell you how happy I am that a professional is finally taking this seriously," wrote Celeste, a homemaker, with two children, who had become hooked on the Internet's chat rooms, spending 60 hours a week in a fanasty on-line world. "My husband argues with me about it. I'm never there for my kids. I'm horrified at how I'm acting, but I just can't seem to stop."

Not surprisingly, a few critics questioned the legitimacy of Internet addiction. A *Newsweek* article titled "Breathing Is Also Addictive" urged readers to "Forget those scare stories about being hooked on the Internet. The Web is not a habit; it's an indelible feature of modern life." The founder of an on-line Internet addiction support group, psychiatrist Ivan K. Goldberg, revealed that he meant it as a joke. But most media accounts, along with a growing number of therapists and addiction counselors, have acknowledged that being addicted to the Internet is no laughing matter.

No one understands the seriousness of the addiction better than the families of Internet addicts. With each new report of my study, I hear from dozens of concerned family members. They contact me by e-mail or, for those who have not learned how to navigate the Net themselves, by phone, or even by letter, known to Internet regulars as snail mail.

Frustrated, confused, lonely, often desperate, these people confide in me the details of life with an Internet addict. Loved ones describe patterns of secrecy and lies, arguments and broken agreements, often culminating in the day their partner ran off to live with someone he or she knew only through the Internet. Parents tell me the sad stories of daughters or sons who went from straight A's to the brink of failure after discovering chat rooms and interactive games that kept them up all night. Other family members and friends of Internet addicts lament the addict's total loss of interest in once-treasured hobbies, movies, parties, visiting friends, talking over dinner, or almost anything else in what the excessive Internet user would call *RL*, or real life.

With alcoholism, chemical dependency, or addictions like gambling and overeating, the person living with the addict often recognizes the problem and seeks to do something about it much earlier and more readily than the addict. I found the same dynamic at work with the loved ones of Internet addicts. When they tried to talk to the Internet addict about his or her behavior and its consequences, they were met with fierce denial. "No one can be addicted to a machine!" the Internet addict responds. Or perhaps the addict counters: "This is just a hobby and besides, everyone is using it today."

These distressed persons have turned to me for validation and support. I assure them that their feelings are justified, the problem is real, and they are not alone. But they want more direct answers to their most troubling questions: What can they do when they believe someone they love has become addicted to the Internet? What are the warning signs? What should they say to the Internet addict to bring him or her back to reality? Where can they go to seek treatment? Who's going to take them seriously?

Help is only slowly beginning to emerge. Clinics to treat computer/Internet addiction have been launched at Proctor Hospital in Peoria, Illinois, and at McLean Hospital in Belmont, Massachusetts, a major teaching facility of Harvard Medical School. Students at the University of Texas and the University of Maryland now can find counseling or seminars on campus to help them understand and manage their Internet addictions. Information about the problem and even support groups have popped up on-line—although some pundits have likened this to holding an AA meeting in a bar. In response to the interest in my study and the demand for more information, I launched my own Web page: the Center for On-Line Addiction. Designed to provide a quick overview of my research and alert Internet users of the problems I've uncovered, this page was visited by several thousand users in its first year.

But so far, such resources are rare exceptions. Most Internet addicts who admit they have a problem and seek treatment for it aren't yet finding acceptance and support from mental health professionals. Some complain that therapists told them to simply "turn off the computer" when it becomes too much for them. That's like telling an alcoholic to "just say no." And it leaves Internet addicts and their loved ones feeling more confused and alone.

That's where I hope this book will help. In the following chapters, you will learn why the Internet can become addictive, who gets addicted to it, what the addictive behavior looks like, and what to do about it. If you already know or at least suspect that you're an Internet addict, you likely will see yourself in many of the personal stories from Internet users who joined in my worldwide study. You will gain a greater understanding of your own experience and recognize that you are not alone. I'll outline concrete steps that will help you regulate your Internet usage and devise a more balanced place for it in your daily life, and I'll point you toward additional resources to keep you on track. I'll help get you out of the black hole of cyberspace.

If you are the partner, parent, or friend of someone whose life has become fixated on the Internet, this book will alert you to the warning signs and symptoms of Internet addiction so you can better understand the problem and find validation, guidance, and support for your loved one—and for yourself. You know that something serious has entered your life, and you will see your reality reflected in the words and experiences of the families of Internet addicts in this book.

For mental health professionals, this book can serve as a clinical guide that will assist in recognizing the addiction and treating it effectively. When I give lectures to groups of therapists or counselors, I often discover that many don't even know how the Internet works, so it's difficult for them to understand what makes this technology so intoxicating or how to help someone manage usage of it. For the uninformed, it's easy to dismiss the idea of Internet addiction—at every lecture I can count on at least one skeptic saying "No one can get addicted to a *machine*." But as we will see, Internet users become psychologically dependent on the feelings and experiences they get while using that machine, and that's what makes it difficult to control or stop.

Addiction counselors recognize this psychological dependency as it applies to compulsive gambling and overeating. It is my hope that this book will encourage them to expand their addiction recovery programs to specifically address the problems of Internet addicts.

This book also will help counselors and teachers in schools and universities become aware of Internet addiction so they can spot it more quickly and effectively counsel students. As we will see, teenagers and college students are particularly susceptible to the lure of the Internet's chat rooms and interactive games. And when they get hooked and stay up late every night on-line, they lose sleep, fail at school, withdraw socially, and lie to their parents about what's happening. Counselors and teachers can help alert students and their parents to the problem and show them how to deal with it.

In the workplace, both managers and employees will benefit from reading this book by gaining a greater awareness of how Internet addiction surfaces on the job and what to do about it. Workers with Internet access will better understand the addictive pull of browsing Web pages, newsgroups, chat rooms, and personal e-mail messages that may lead them to waste hours of work time without realizing it or intending to do so. Employers will recognize the importance of limiting and monitoring their workers' on-line usage to ensure that the Internet is used properly on the job and does not become a source of diminished productivity or distrust. Human resource managers will be alerted to the need to ask employees who show a sudden rise in fatigue or absenteeism whether they just got a home computer with Internet access and whether they've been staying up late using it.

I also hope that Internet promoters, as well as politicians who trumpet the Internet's rise, will read this book and consider the potential addictive nature of this revolutionary technology. A more thorough understanding of the Internet's many applications and how people actually are using them will help everyone keep a clear and balanced perspective on the Net's attributes and its pitfalls. Similarly, the media can continue to play an important role in balancing the flood of news about the wonders of this new toy with timely reminders about the other side of the story.

And for all those who have not yet joined the Internet generation, you probably have heard that the Internet likely will become as routine a part of your life as television—and soon. So this is the best time to learn what to expect on-line and the danger signals that could lead you toward Internet overuse. You are in the best position to learn how to *use* the Internet and not *abuse* it.

Let me be clear about my own position. I certainly don't regard the Internet as an evil villain that can destroy our way of life. In no way do I advocate getting rid of the Internet or stopping its development. I recognize and applaud its many benefits in searching for information, keeping up with the latest news, and communicating with others rapidly and efficiently. Indeed, when I need to begin a new research project, the Internet is often my first stop.

My goal is to help ensure that while we're still in a relatively early phase of Internet expansion, we see and understand the full picture. We're bombarded with cultural messages that urge us to welcome this new tool, and we're assured that it will only improve and enrich our lives. It has that capability. But it also has an addictive potential with harmful consequences that, left undetected and unchecked, could silently run rampant in our schools, our universities, our offices, our libraries, and our homes. By becoming informed and aware, we can best chart ways for the Internet to *connect* us rather than *disconnect* us from one another.

Clearly, the Internet is here to stay. But as we all head out onto the information superhighway together, let's at least make sure we have a clear view of the road ahead and our seat belts securely fastened.

## ONE

# The Dark Side
# of Cyberspace

*I get tongue-tied in real life, but I don't get finger-tied on the Net.* —A 38-YEAR-OLD WOMAN FROM CHICAGO ADDICTED TO CHAT ROOMS

L et me take you on a tour of the "other side" of the Internet. On this tour, you won't hear President Clinton insist that every child in every classroom must be hooked up to the Internet for Americans to raise their standard of education and stay competitive in the global economy. You won't be harassed by advertisements that invite you to "visit us on the World Wide Web." You won't be encouraged to utilize the ease and convenience of doing all your banking and shopping from the comfort of your home computer. You won't learn Howard Stern's personal on-line address. And after you watch the TV news or read your newspaper, you won't be told how to find the latest breaking news on the Internet.

We're headed instead for the dark side of cyberspace. You'll be meeting the men, women, and children who have emerged through my research on Internet addiction. Caught in an on-line underworld of nonstop chat rooms, fantasy dungeons of monsters and mayhem, and electronic bulletin boards with more listings than a small city's telephone directory, these Internet addicts are engrossed in a very different experience than the one you might imagine exists for eager learners and dedicated information seekers. Internet addicts' confessions suggest that there's a different dimension to the same Internet you see glorified in the mass media every day. Rather than becoming the technological savior of our times, the Internet just might be emerging as the addiction of the millennium, surpassing even TV with its pervasive grip on our minds and souls.

As you begin, you'll be moving along this opposite lane of the information superhighway at a pace that simulates the rapid-fire speed of cyberspace. You'll catch glimpses of these Internet junkies and their families, and get an idea of the problems they encounter. Later in this chapter, and throughout the book, you'll learn much more about Internet addicts—who they are, why they get hooked, the damage the addiction causes, what sucks them into cyberspace, and how they can climb out. The Internet Addiction Test at the end of this chapter will help you or your loved one determine whether you're already hooked.

## THE ON-LINE UNDERWORLD

But first the tour, which kicks off with the word that triggers any action on-line:

*Click.*

Bob, a 38-year-old auto mechanic from New Jersey, gets lost in Internet Usenet groups. He spends most leisure hours reading and answering postings on everything from business and politics to auto repair and bartending. When his wife and two children invite him along on a weekend camping trip or even to a movie, he tells them to go on without him. Son Josh, 13, pleads with his dad to shoot baskets with him in the driveway. "Can't you see I'm busy?" Bob snaps. Bob once got so immersed in typing car repair advice to a "friend" in the Midwest that he forgot to pick up 11-year-old daughter Tracy at school. "I don't mean to spend all my time this way, but I can't stop," Bob sighed. "It's the one place my opinion matters and I feel important."

*Click.*

Mary Lou juggles a home-based boutique in a small North Carolina town with primary caretaking of her four children under age 12. As a late-night regular of Internet chat rooms, she stays up until 5 A.M. She's falling behind in her housework, her cooking, and her business. And while she swaps endless stories of her day with her chat-room pals, she ignores her husband and children. "I feel guilty about it, but when I tried to break free, I simply didn't have the strength to turn the computer off and leave it off," Mary Lou lamented. "I'm a longtime cigarette smoker, but I've found the craving to go on the Internet first thing every morning is stronger than my urge to light a cigarette!"

*Click.*

Christine gained Internet access as part of her job as an administrative assistant in a busy real estate office. But instead of streamlining her work communication, she cruised the relationship groups—the singles ads of cyberspace—and "met" a man she liked. They typed love messages back and forth throughout the workday. When Christine's boss caught on, he cut off her Internet privileges and gave her an official warning. "So I convinced a friend at work to let me borrow her Internet account," she confessed. "When my boss found out, he fired me on the spot."

*Click.*

Brenda has been married to Eric for 10 years. They got along fine until Brenda discovered chat rooms. Now she only steps out of the computer room to go to the bathroom or get something out of the refrigerator, and when she comes to bed, Eric's been asleep for hours. They argue about this constantly. "I even tried to get him to use the computer just to stop the fighting, but he wanted nothing to do with it," Brenda explained. "He wants me to give up the Internet, but I need it too much in my life. When it comes right down to it, I won't give it up—not even for him."

*Click.*

Tony, a recently married construction worker, rushes home every night to go on-line to slay monsters and dragons and beat up opponents in the interactive game DOOM-II. "By day, I am a mild-mannered husband and dedicated worker," Tony told me, "but by night, with a click of the button, I turn into the most aggressive bastard you can imagine. And no one knows it's me doing this. I think it keeps me from actually hurting people— like beating my wife. It's scary to me. I need help with this."

*Click.*

Rick, a recovering alcoholic, was recently laid off from his manufacturing job. Home alone all day while his wife, Leslie, works, he spends eight hours surfing the Web instead of studying the help wanted ads. When Leslie gets home and asks him how long he spent on the computer, he says two hours maximum. "It's just like when she used to ask me how many beers I had during the day. I'd say two when I really drank a six-pack," Rick admitted. "I lied then to avoid the hassle, and I lie now to avoid the same hassle."

*Click.*

Seventeen-year-old Jennifer was a straight-A high school student when she gave in to the lure of the adolescent-geared chat rooms, where she would share her fears and insecurities for 100 hours or more per month. Within a year, her grades had tumbled, she had withdrawn from her real-life friends and family, and she began complaining of

symptoms of several diseases that doctors could not identify. Her mother, Nancy, believes Jennifer fell prey to the
suggestions of her new Internet friends. At 18 she left
home to live with a group of them. "I'm at a loss as to
which way to turn," Nancy confided. "I've tried social services, our church, her school. No one seems to know how
to deal with this Internet addiction and what happens to
kids there."

## THE ADDICTION AND THE DAMAGE DONE

The examples just presented illustrate clearly that Internet addicts, like alcoholics or drug addicts, suffer major
problems in the main categories of everyday life: *family,
work, relationships, school.*

In the family arena, Mary Lou is neglecting her husband and four kids, Bob's children can't get through to
him, and Jennifer disappeared so far into the black hole
of cyberspace that her mother worries that she won't get
her back. At work, Christine got so engrossed in chat
rooms that she got fired.

In the relationship realm, Brenda's dependence on
the Internet is so strong that she's choosing her on-line
world over her 10-year marriage, and Tony fears that the
monster he becomes playing interactive games may be
unleashed as violence against his wife. At school, Internet
abuse sabotaged Jennifer's former standing as a straight-
A high school student. A college student from my study
told me that he fears flunking out because that would
mean losing his free, unrestricted, 24-hour-a-day Internet
access!

Looking further, we can see how Internet addicts try to
cover up evidence of their habit in order to maintain it,
just as alcoholics or drug addicts do. Rick recognized that
he was lying to his wife about his Internet usage the same

way he had deceived her about his drinking. When Christine's employer cut off her source of Internet use, she snuck off to gain access to her friend's on-line account.

The comparison to other addictions cuts even deeper. Bob admits that he spends much longer periods on-line than he intended, like an alcoholic drinking more than he wants to or even can remember. Mary Lou compares the craving for the Internet to the urge for a cigarette, and her habit is so severe that she can't stop when she tries. She's losing all control over her Internet usage, and her life. Those are clear indicators of addiction at work.

Brenda and Bob are withdrawing from those around them to hang out with their friends on the Internet, much as alcoholics prefer the company of fellow drinkers who will support them in their addictive behavior. And many Internet users who try to quit cold turkey speak of withdrawal symptoms comparable to those hooked on physical substances. Kenny, a 16-year-old brought to a drug and alcohol treatment center by his parents to help him curb his destructive Internet habits, got so nervous, shaky, and angry from being denied access to a computer that he began throwing chairs and banging tables.

And yet, the Internet is not a substance ingested into the body. That's what confuses many Internet addicts who simply don't recognize or want to admit that they've become hooked. The Internet is just part of a computer, they argue, and you can't get addicted to a simple object. In the last two decades, psychologists and addiction counselors have begun to acknowledge that people can form addictions to more than physical substances. They point to common *addictive behavior* in such habits as compulsive gambling, chronic overeating, sexual compulsions, and obsessive television watching. In behavior-oriented addictions, those who get hooked are addicted to what they *do* and the *feelings* they experience when they're doing it. That's how it works for Internet addicts.

## NEW FRIENDS, NEW LIFE

Consider Jeanne, a 34-year-old wife and homemaker from South Carolina. By appearances, Jeanne had a perfect life: an attentive husband, a nice house, two healthy toddlers, a few good friends through her church.

Her relationship with the Internet began innocently enough. She tried the chat rooms out of curiosity and met a few new friends, mostly other women who stayed at home during the day. Conversation flowed easily, and she found that if she felt just a bit lonely or stressed from keeping up with the kids, she had a ready-made, always-available circle of allies to call upon for comfort and supportive listening. Because most of her real friends from church worked during the day, Jeanne found chat rooms especially appealing. As an added bonus, she didn't have to worry about what she looked like when one or more of these Internet friends "dropped by" to visit, as the following excerpt illustrates:

> *Good afternoon! I am waiting for my bread to bake at the moment, which means I've got time to kill. I do this every few weeks because I like to have something else to keep my eye on during the day than all those soaps on TV! Wouldn't you just love to be here to smell that sweet aroma? Then again, you probably wouldn't wish to see me in my old flannel robe and slippers with the holes in the soles. It's 1 P.M. and I haven't even taken my morning shower. If a salesperson came to the door, I'd want to die (lol) [cyberspeak for laughing out loud]. Even my husband and my two boys are not allowed to see me in this condition. I hope you know what I mean. Anyway, this down time gives me the perfect opportunity to send an e-mail in your direction.*

Jeanne was having fun, more fun than watching soaps because she was engaged in actual interactions with "real" people. What these Internet friends didn't know was that Jeanne is 50 pounds overweight, a source of great shame for her. The fun grew more serious as she grew closer to these women and began sharing her most personal thoughts and intimate details of her life. They, not her husband or real-life friends, became her confidantes. And as she looked forward to each new day of chatting, they became her life.

"I felt attractive, interesting, and more at ease," Jeanne said of her chat-room experiences. "These are feelings I had never experienced in my life."

Although Jeanne's husband, Tom, didn't know the full nature of his wife's on-line relationships, he knew how much time she was spending there from the bills for their on-line service. And he could easily detect the changes in Jeanne's behavior. She became more preoccupied and withdrawn, and much less affectionate. When he came home from work and dinner wasn't ready the way it used to be, he'd get angry and call her an addict. She got defensive. Maybe she's just lonely, Tom thought, and it's a phase that will pass. When his friends complained that they could never reach him because the phone was always busy (from Jeanne's on-line connection), Tom was too ashamed to admit the truth. He put in another phone line for Jeanne's modem.

As Jeanne's addictive behavior got worse, her on-line time began encroaching into their formerly shared evening hours. She refused to go out to dinner with Tom because that would mean sacrificing time in the chat rooms. Soon she even stopped cooking, cleaning, and doing the laundry. And she met a new friend in the chat rooms—Fred.

Fred made Jeanne laugh. He always seemed to understand her moods, especially when she shared her sadness and regret over her choice to marry Tom at 19, before she had a chance to explore other relationships. He offered her support and encouragement, more than she had ever imagined a man could offer. Then he started asking about her sexual fantasies, and he revealed his own. That led to the exchange of erotic messages—*cybersex.* Next, they swapped pictures electronically and soon arranged a real-life rendezvous. Within weeks, Jeanne filed for divorce. Through the Internet, she had formed a bond so close that she tossed aside a 15-year marriage.

## THE SEDUCTIVE LURE OF CYBERSPACE

As Jeanne's story indicates, the Internet is truly alive, a living, breathing electronic community. For obsessive Internet users it's a second home, a special place where they feel they belong. Like the old TV show *Cheers,* the Internet becomes the place where everybody knows your name—or at least your "handle," which is the name and persona you choose to go by.

For many lonely users like Jeanne, this second home becomes more appealing than their real-life home. They become hooked on what they do and find there, dependent on the feelings they experience in this virtual community. It may be the only time they feel so free and uninhibited, so cared for and desired, so connected with others. Naturally, then, they want to use the Internet more and more to capture those good feelings and bring them into their day-to-day existence. As they chase after what stirs their deepest desires, they easily can feel tempted to kiss their old home good-bye.

Not all Internet addicts are plotting to run away and start a new life, of course. But throughout my three-year study of this phenomenon, I've found that some form of escape usually lies at the heart and soul of the drive toward Internet addiction. Many of these people are depressed and lonely, held back by low self-esteem, insecurity, and anxiety. Maybe they're unhappy in their relationships, or their jobs, or their social life. A few are battling diseases like cancer, or living with a permanent disability. Teenagers who succumb to the Internet's pull often say they're misunderstood by their parents and feel trapped at home.

But with the Internet, they seemingly can get away from it all. They escape into a fantasyland where they make instant friends and talk any time of the day and night. From the safety of one's bedroom, office, or dorm, this electronic community emerges with remarkable ease. You don't have to get dressed up, check yourself in the mirror, or drive anywhere to meet your on-line companions. And unlike an earlier generation's experience with pen pals, you don't have to wait days or weeks for a response. With every message you type, you instantly connect with fellow users all over the world. They say something witty or provocative, you immediately answer in kind. Soon you're typing words you wouldn't dream of saying in your real life, where you may be inhibited by how people might react. In the safe haven of cyberspace, you share your deepest feelings, offer your strongest opinions, and reach out to people much faster and more openly than you would in real life.

The other people in this make-believe world can't see you, and they don't know who you are. You can be whomever you choose, act however you want. If you're shy in real life, you can become outgoing on the Internet. If you're dull at a party, you can be witty in cyberspace. As one woman explained: "I can get tongue-tied in real life, but I don't get finger-tied on the Net."

If you're cautious by nature, you can take chances in cyberspace. If you're considered unattractive and overweight by people who meet you in person, with a little artistic license on the Internet you can become younger and more alluring. To borrow from Garrison Keillor's description of Lake Wobegon, the Internet community becomes the place where all the women are assertive and adventuresome, all the men are blond, 25-year-old hunks, and all the children are wonderfully creative and mature beyond their years.

These Internet addicts, clearly, do not regard the Net as simply an informational or communication tool, nor do they use it simply for enjoyment. To them, it's a form of escape that allows them to forget their problems for the time they spend on-line, much like the numbing sensation alcoholics report when they drink.

The downside, however, is that the escape is temporary. When the Internet addict finally logs off for the night, the screen goes dark on the fantasy world. Real-life problems return, and now they're even harder to endure. Depression deepens, loneliness intensifies, and there's the added burden of guilt for neglecting spouse or family. That propels addicts into going on-line even more often for even longer periods of time—to find a panacea for the awakened painful feelings and to chase after the "high" they remembered from their last walk through a chat room or newsgroup.

This is the same cycle known to alcoholics: drink to escape their problems; feel worse afterward; drink more to wipe away those worsening feelings. Similarly, compulsive gamblers often start betting to escape their unhappy lives and economic difficulties. They feel temporary relief from the high that comes from the hope of winning the bet at the track or hitting the lottery jackpot, fed by an occasional payoff. Then the problems of real life come rushing back to the front, along with guilt for throwing away money and amassing greater debts, which leads to a stronger need to escape into betting.

## MINDTHRILL

But the lure of cyberspace reaches well beyond a desire to escape. The appeal of an electronic world without limits is multidimensional. For computer lovers, the Internet dazzles the senses with its immense power and capabilities to connect and communicate. That's how Dave experiences it. He's been tinkering with computers since he was seven years old, and his work in the telecommunications center of a military base keeps him in touch with the latest technology. He spends hundreds of dollars every month on the newest software and technological wizardry, and with his expertise he's not easily impressed. But the Internet has penetrated all circuits of his brain and emotions.

"When you're talking about the Internet, you're talking about power. It's the most powerful information tool I have ever known," Dave told me. "When I explore the on-line world, I feel like that robot in the movie *Short Circuit*. I need more input! More input!"

Dave is tingling from the experience of what I call mindthrill, the Internet's constant stimulation of the senses with a cornucopia of electronic delights. If you're drawn to the Net for information, you'll find avenues of facts, opinions, statistics, and data that seldom seem routine. If you took all the channels from the most extensive cable TV system and multiplied it by 50, you still wouldn't come close to matching the sources of information that lay before you on the Net. Some information-hungry Internet addicts told me they're so wired from what they see while sitting in front of the computer that they want to climb inside their terminal.

"I feel the rush every time my mind gets connected to this intensely powerful information whirlpool," explains Josh, a 29-year-old computer programmer. "When I enter cyberspace, I become one with my mind. It's like Mr. Spock doing the Vulcan Mindmeld."

## INSTANT VIRTUOSO

Of course, you need not have grown up as a computer whiz like Dave or Josh to fully experience the magnetism of mindthrill. Any Internet user can be hooked by the power, stimulation, and excitement of going on-line. Browsing thousands of Web pages on your favorite subject can capture your mind's full attention, even if you haven't a clue about the technological mechanisms that make it all possible. And if you're an Internet user in Pennsylvania who's never traveled west of the Mississippi River, the first chat-room message from someone in England, or even in Idaho, can entice you with the wonder of stepping into a worldwide melting pot from your own home.

You don't even need a long history of computer experience and knowledge to learn your way around the Internet. Many survey respondents told me they had been living as computer-phobics for years until someone introduced them to the Internet. When they discovered the logic of the Internet's organization, they found navigating the Net simpler than programming their VCR. Indeed, the quick and easy mastery of the Internet becomes part of the allure. If you didn't believe you could ever conquer a computer, and within a few weeks you're casually pulling up all the background information on the actor you liked in a movie 15 years ago, you begin to fancy yourself as a young Mozart, mastering your new instrument while still a cyberchild.

## EMOTIONAL NURTURANCE

If your surfing lands you in the Net's chat rooms, the temporary emotional benefits may seduce you into forming deeper attachments. As we saw with Jeanne, the people you encounter in the chat rooms appear to offer not only companionship, but also the kind of caring, support, and encouragement that often takes years to cultivate in a real-life friendship. Even in the aggressive interactive games, participants tend to compete against the same players for weeks or months on end, so deep bonds form. In cyberspace, connections are formed as quickly as time zones are crossed. And those real-life friends who expect more than a few typed messages of caring suddenly don't seem so important.

"When I'm with my real friends, I'm always thinking about my chat-room friends," admitted Internet regular Susan. "But when I'm with my chat-room friends, I never think of my real friends. One day, one of my chat-room friends told me she was going to stop talking to me. I cried for days, and I kept replaying our electronic conversations over and over."

Even when you're not forming deep emotional bonds with every Net stranger you bump into at 2 A.M., your Internet family can appear to serve a multitude of critical needs. Sometimes Internet users simply get on-line to vent their common daily frustrations, without expecting feedback from anyone who "listens in" on another computer screen somewhere far away. If you're still angry with your boyfriend about something he did last weekend, you can type your feelings about it the same way you might write a letter that you never intend to send. If you had a fight with your boss and you don't want to worry your wife with all the details, you can explode on-line with no repercussions (except in that unlikely event that your boss is logged on to the same chat room).

Internet users say this form of venting satisfies them more fully than previous coping strategies like watching violent TV shows and vicariously acting out their emotions through the characters. On the Internet, you are the character acting out your own feelings, and it doesn't hurt to know that you've got a captive audience out there.

Internet users who join discussion groups on politics, business, or religion enjoy the freedom to express their deepest convictions and strongest opinions about whatever topic is on the board. You don't actually see anyone's physical response to your messages—no facial expressions that say you're weird, no shaking of the head that tells you you're stupid or naive. Even if someone types a response to your opinion that you don't like, you simply ignore it and wait for the next message from a more affirming source. Then you feel the kind of instant validation and recognition that's tough to count on in most social situations.

Father John, a priest active and well respected in his parish, disagrees with aspects of the Catholic faith, such as not allowing women to be priests and mandatory celibacy. Yet he would never voice his reservations publicly to his congregation. But in the *alt.recovery.catholicism* discussion group, he openly states his opinions without fear of retribution. Those who share his views comfort the priest, and those who challenge him allow him an opportunity to debate these issues without ever having to reveal his vocation and true identity.

It's a bit like talk radio. You call up and lambast the politicians you most detest, with strong arguments and witty insults, then five minutes later another caller from across the country calls in to agree with you. You feel smart that you're tuned in to popular viewpoints.

But on the Internet, the interaction is two-way and immediate. Instead of listening to two callers agreeing with you in the next hour after your call on talk radio, you get dozens of affirming and validating remarks in the next two minutes. And when you find someone on your same wavelength, you can invite them to a private corner of the discussion room and talk back to them, which opens the door to discover where else you two click. Your self-esteem rises. Like Bob from our initial tour, you may come to feel that the Internet is the only place you feel important and valued for your ideas and intelligence.

## A WEB OF MYSTERY

Internet usage is rising rapidly. One survey completed in December 1997 revealed that the on-line community had expanded to 56 million people, an increase of 4.9 million new users within the past three months. How many of those users are addicted already? If we base our estimate on the accepted range of 5 to 10 percent of all users used to estimate the number of those addicted to alcohol or gambling, we would be led to conclude that over 5 million Internet users are addicted today.

But those established addictions have been around much longer, and many people may spend years in occasional drug or alcohol use before becoming ensnared in addictive patterns. Not so with the Internet. I found that 25 percent of all respondents reported getting hooked in their first 6 months on-line. An additional 58 percent had met my criteria for addiction within six months to a year of their Internet initiation. The remaining 17 percent didn't become addicted until after their first year on-line. With so many users becoming addicted so soon after their initial log-in, the actual number of Internet addicts already may be considerably higher—and soaring upward every day.

This reality powerfully challenges our assumptions. When you walk by the college computer lab late at night and see hundreds of students rapidly typing away on their keyboards, you're tempted to conclude that they're gathering research information or writing and rewriting papers. The truth is, a large percentage of them are gossiping in chat rooms and blowing up monsters in interactive games, like teenagers in a video arcade at the mall.

When you see your husband retire to the den after dinner for four hours on-line, you want to believe he's following up on that important project from work. The truth is he may be sharing intimate details of your life together with another woman or even engaging in cybersex—an affair with no paper trail or threat of disease. When you see your employee apparently studying the Web pages of your competitors, the truth may be that she's chatting with on-line friends about the weather, her social life, and your unfair treatment of her in the office. When you buy separate modems for your two children to allow each to work on their homework in their own rooms, you may unwittingly be opening the door to marathon chat sessions that lead to declining grades, secret plots to run away with a cyberfriend, and a disconnection of family life more destructive than stationing individual TV sets in every room of the house.

Of course, millions of nonaddicts do use the Internet today to enhance their lives. Even playing in the chat rooms or with interactive games now and then can be harmless fun—if it's not done to excess or does not cause problems in real life. But it's now quite clear that the dark side of cyberspace is not limited to a tiny corner of the basement. It's permeated our entire culture.

## A MILLENNIAL ADDICTION

When we consider our circumstances as we near century's end, the emergence of Internet addiction today really should not surprise us. For one thing, we live in an era that celebrates technology. Computer mavericks such as Bill Gates have become models of creative imagination and business acumen. Each new technological development is hailed as a tool that will better prepare us for the twenty-first century, with the Internet leading the way. It's natural that people feel compelled to check it out, and once on-line to overindulge in the technological smorgasbord.

We're also driven by a fast-food mentality that demands immediate delivery of anything we want, coupled with the ability to instantly leave behind anything we find boring or tiresome. The rapid clicking of the TV remote was simply good practice for the even more rapid clicking of the mouse. With today's prevalence of such passive pursuits as spectator sports, soap operas, and virtual reality, we've become accustomed to involvement at a distance. The Net is a vicarious paradise, entered without any walking, driving, flying, or even dialing the phone. The couch potato of the '80s has become the mouse potato of the '90s.

The Internet also attracts us as an antidote for our general cultural malaise. We see the breakup of family and community, as well as mounting evidence of isolation and fear, and cynicism. Going on-line can connect us to a new family that at least appears to offer what our real families can't. And the Internet community that welcomes us to our new home is thousands of times larger than the neighborhood block parties of a bygone era. Your cyberspace friends won't be making any insulting remarks about the color of your carpet, either.

If we feel powerless against crime, greed, corruption, and our economic struggles, we can tap into the limitless power of the information superhighway. If we feel isolated, we can pour out all our repressed feelings and act out hidden aspects of ourselves in meeting rooms and interactive games. If we long for love and affection but fear rejection or AIDS, we can cruise for cybersex. And if we're bored with our family or cynical about our society, we can retreat into a subculture of Internet addicts who offer support, encouragement, excitement and intrigue, and maybe even an invitation to come run away from it all.

Unhappiness creates a natural breeding ground for addictions. The Internet has tapped into that source. And because the conditions are ripe for addictive behavior throughout our culture and our world, Internet addicts cut across age, gender, social, educational, and economic lines. An Internet addict can be your best friend, your own child, your parent, your partner, or your employee. An Internet addict could be the local bank's president or its custodian, the public school principal or an average student. Or you!

## ARE YOU AN INTERNET ADDICT?

How do you know if you're already addicted or tumbling toward trouble? Everyone's situation is different, and it's not simply a matter of time spent on-line. Some respondents to my survey indicated they were addicted with only 20 hours per week of Internet use, while others who spend 40 hours per week on-line insisted it was not a problem to them, and their answers did not fit the criteria for established addictions. It's more important to measure the damage your Internet use causes in your life. What conflicts have emerged in family, relationships, work, or school—similar to the problems we've seen in this chapter?

The following test will help in three ways: (1) If you already know or strongly believe you are addicted to the Internet, this test will assist you in identifying the areas in your life most impacted by your excessive Net use; (2) if you're not sure whether you're addicted, this test will help determine the answer and begin to assess the damage done; and (3) if you suspect or fear that someone you know may be addicted to the Internet, you can give that person this test to find out.

## INTERNET ADDICTION TEST

To assess your level of addiction, answer the following questions using this scale:

1 = Not at all
2 = Rarely
3 = Occasionally
4 = Often
5 = Always

1. How often do you find that you stay on-line longer than you intended?
   1    2    3    4    5
2. How often do you neglect household chores to spend more time on-line?
   1    2    3    4    5
3. How often do you prefer the excitement of the Internet to intimacy with your partner?
   1    2    3    4    5
4. How often do you form new relationships with fellow on-line users?
   1    2    3    4    5
5. How often do others in your life complain to you about the amount of time you spend on-line?
   1    2    3    4    5
6. How often do your grades or school work suffer because of the amount of time you spend on-line?
   1    2    3    4    5
7. How often do you check your e-mail before something else that you need to do?
   1    2    3    4    5

*continued on page 32*

8.  How often does your job performance or productivity suffer because of the Internet?
    1     2     3     4     5

9.  How often do you become defensive or secretive when anyone asks you what you do on-line?
    1     2     3     4     5

10. How often do you block out disturbing thoughts about your life with soothing thoughts of the Internet?
    1     2     3     4     5

11. How often do you find yourself anticipating when you will go on-line again?
    1     2     3     4     5

12. How often do you fear that life without the Internet would be boring, empty, and joyless?
    1     2     3     4     5

13. How often do you snap, yell, or act annoyed if someone bothers you while you are on-line?
    1     2     3     4     5

14. How often do you lose sleep due to late-night log-ins?
    1     2     3     4     5

15. How often do you feel preoccupied with the Internet when off-line, or fantasize about being on-line?
    1     2     3     4     5

16. How often do you find yourself saying "just a few more minutes" when on-line?
    1     2     3     4     5

17. How often do you try to cut down the amount of time you spend on-line and fail?
    1     2     3     4     5

18. How often do you try to hide how long you've been on-line?
    1     2     3     4     5

*continued on page 33*

*INTERNET ADDICTION QUIZ, continued from page 32*

19. How often do you choose to spend more time on-line over going out with others?

    1    2    3    4    5

20. How often do you feel depressed, moody, or nervous when you are off-line, which goes away once you are back on-line?

    1    2    3    4    5

After you've answered all the questions, add the numbers you selected for each response to obtain a final score. The higher your score, the greater your level of addiction and the problems your Internet usage causes. Here's a general scale to help measure your score.

**20–39 points:** You are an average on-line user. You may surf the Web a bit too long at times, but you have control over your usage.

**40–69 points:** You are experiencing frequent problems because of the Internet. You should consider their full impact on your life.

**70–100 points:** Your Internet usage is causing significant problems in your life. You need to address them now.

After you have identified the category that fits your total score, look back at those questions for which you scored a 4 or 5. Did you realize this was a significant problem for you? For example, if you answered 4 (often) to Question #2 regarding your neglect of household chores, were you aware of just how often your dirty laundry piles up or how empty the refrigerator gets?

Say you answered 5 (always) to Question #14 about lost sleep due to late-night log-ins. Have you ever stopped to think about how hard it has become to drag yourself out of bed every morning? Do you feel exhausted at work? Has this pattern begun to take its toll on your body and your overall health?

In the chapters ahead, I'll show you how to address these problems caused by your Internet use and help you gain a greater understanding of their roots. If you scored over 70 on the test, you are in particular need of this information. If you found yourself in the gray area with a score of 40 to 69, I'll help you begin to zero in on the areas of greatest concern to you. Together, we'll construct a new program to a better way of living, both on-line and off. And if you scored in the 20 to 39 range, indicating that you only occasionally spend too much time with the Internet, you'll learn simple time-management techniques to help you regain control over the clock. The ground we cover along the way will be equally as useful to parents, partners, and friends of Internet addicts.

Suppose you only recently discovered the Internet and you found that many of the questions don't seem particularly relevant to you. If you're reading this book, you've probably wondered if you might be prone to Internet addiction down the line. This is the best time to learn of the danger signals and the potential damage from excessive use. Like Luke Skywalker in *Star Wars,* if you learn about the dark side right from the start of your Internet training, you have a far better chance of not giving in to it later. So let's continue on a deeper exploration of this new galaxy that's as close as your school, office, or home.

# TWO

# The Terminal Time Warp

*It's like being in high school! Twenty-three best friends talking all night long.* — *"BETH," A PSYCHOTHERAPY CLIENT QUOTED IN THE* FAMILY THERAPY NETWORKER

Robin prides herself on her discipline. A 29-year-old public relations consultant, she works hard and takes care of herself: healthy food, regular exercise; plenty of rest. Until recently she went to bed at 10 P.M. every night to make sure she'd get her full eight hours sleep before her alarm rang at 6 A.M. That left her plenty of time for her morning jog and a leisurely breakfast before heading off to work at 7:45.

A few months ago, Robin subscribed to America On-line and quickly discovered chat rooms. The first few times she only visited for an hour or so, finding the chat rooms a pleasant diversion. But then she stumbled upon a few groups of people who sounded more like her, and she began to engage in fascinating discussions about business, travel, movies, photography, and relationships. So much for discipline.

"Now I stay up until at least 2 A.M. every night," she admits. "I never intend to stay on that long, but every night it's the same."

In the morning, Robin hits the snooze button on her alarm several times before dragging herself out of bed. There's no time for morning jogs, and those leisurely breakfasts are gone, replaced by the bagel she grabs as she runs out the door. She arrives at work exhausted, and those bursts of creativity that once flowed easily on the job when her mind was fresh and clear seldom come to her anymore. Where she used to limit herself to two cups of coffee in the morning, now she needs six or seven just to get her through to lunch. When she staggers home, she knows that she should go to bed early to catch up on her rest, but by 8:30 P.M. she's back in cyberspace, where she quickly forgets those rational ideas about sleep.

"One time," Robin recalls, "I stayed on-line so long that I heard the birds singing and could see the sun rising out my window before I realized it was 6 A.M.—time to get up."

Robin got caught in the Terminal Time Warp, a phenomenon that almost all Internet users experience at some point in their on-line travels. Whether it's searching a couple of hundred Web sites for that one recipe you know you had seen before; answering the 50 messages in your e-mail box, or debating whether the differences between men and women are genetic or environmental, it's common to lose all track of time. And when someone or something prompts you to take stock of how much time has slipped by on the Internet, you're jolted by the reality. Four hours? Seemed like only 15 minutes.

If you're like most Internet users, you recognize this common symptom. Whether serious Internet addict or relatively casual browser, you've probably had moments of total surprise, coupled with embarrassment or even alarm at how much time you consumed when you went on-line for "a few minutes." In my survey, *97 percent* of all respondents reported that they found themselves spending longer periods of time on-line than they intended.

Look back at Question #1 of the Internet Addiction Test in the previous chapter: *How often do you find that you stay on-line longer than you intended?* If you answered "often" or "always," you are typical of the women, men, and teenagers I've been interviewing. And even if you answered "occasionally" or "rarely," you probably still have felt humbled by how quickly and easily you can get lost in cyberspace. Maybe you've wondered what you can do to make sure it doesn't happen more frequently. Let's explore this Terminal Time Warp and consider the following:

- How does time slip by so quickly when you're using the Internet, and what makes it so difficult to notice it?
- Why do you get sidetracked more easily on the Internet than when you're reading a novel that you can't put down?
- What are you losing, other than sleep, when you continue to get caught in the time warp?
- What long-term consequences threaten to impact your life in "real" time?
- How can you manage your on-line time, using the Internet for your intended purposes without sabotaging your basic life needs?

## A BOOK WITHOUT AN ENDING

Whatever the initial reason for venturing on-line, people soon learn that finding what they want and getting out is seldom as quick and easy as opening the refrigerator door and grabbing a snack. Joey, a high school senior who considers himself an accomplished navigator on the World Wide Web, recently turned to the Net after watching Howard Stern's movie *Private Parts*. He was searching for information on the character Jackie "The Joke Man" Martling, and he estimated that it would take him five minutes to find it.

He began at Stern's Web page, http://www.private-parts.com. From there, Joey had to weed through dozens of audio and video clips of the movie, which he stopped to appreciate because he had enjoyed the movie so much. He even found several still photos from the film. A side route led him to bios of every significant cast member. Next, he landed in the middle of several discussion groups about the movie, and of course he needed to offer his opinion. Finally, Joey arrived at his final destination, seven links and 45 minutes after he set out on this simple Web journey.

On the Web, anyone is free to build his or her own page, and no one is providing any quality control. When you're surfing, you're as likely to bump into Howard Stern or Bill Clinton as you are of landing on a page created by a teenager tinkering in his bedroom. It's a crowded field, and even with helpful information-sorting systems such as Netscape, it takes patience, persistence, and time to trudge through the garbage swirling in the whirlpool of info glut. You may get lost for a while, but you grow more determined to fight your way through. And with dazzling graphics and impressive titles, even Internet trash has a certain appeal that lures you for a five-minute peek. By the time you find what you were looking for, you're often so entranced by the vastness of cyberspace that you want to embark on a new informational journey right away.

Even the most disciplined visitors get lured into exploring more of the Net's endless possibilities. Scott, a warehouse manager from the Midwest, recently landed a new job in New York City. Feeling intimidated about finding a place to live there, he heard that he could actually call up New York apartment listings on his home computer. It took him awhile to find his way around, but once he got used to it, Scott welcomed this on-line search as infinitely quieter, safer, and calmer than trying to master the New York subway system.

After targeting several apartment prospects, he followed the Internet trail that urged him to click onto the names of real estate agents who could instantly line up appointments for him to check out apartments the day he arrived in New York. One agent then pointed him to the spot on the Internet where he could take a virtual tour of the city. Soon he was spending hours "climbing" the Empire State Building, "shopping" along Fifth Avenue, "hanging out" in Greenwich Village, and "attending" Broadway plays.

Dazzled by the capability and diversity of the Web, as most *newbies* (newcomers) usually are in their first few weeks, Scott heard about following sports on-line. He soon learned that with a bit of on-line searching he could access more scores, statistics, highlights, player profiles, and trade rumors than he'd find in a year's subscription to *Sports Illustrated.* He switched on the Net to chronicle the statistics of Cal Ripken, his favorite player. Then he began tracing the box scores of every World Series in the past 50 years. An Internet investment that began with five hours a week when he first scanned New York apartment listings had quickly grown to a 25-hour-a-week habit.

I've experienced for myself how any Internet user can become completely absorbed and easily sidetracked. I use the Internet regularly in my professional life, with my own Web page outlining my Internet addiction study, and e-mail communication with addicts, their families, and the many therapists and academicians who want information about my research findings. I also go on-line seeking ideas or research leads for the classes I teach at the University of Pittsburgh at Bradford.

One day, about two hours before class, I was looking over *The Chronicle of Higher Education's* Web page when I spotted a relevant item on a researcher from the University of Chicago. I looked up that faculty person's credentials. That led me to another link offering an attractive picture of the campus, then another that pictured the city surrounding the campus, and several intriguing web sites about Chicago's businesses. When I finally glanced at my watch, I blurted out: "Oh no, I'm late for class!" I rushed in 10 minutes late, relieved to find that my students hadn't given up and walked out on me.

Time seems to stand still on the Internet because no one's measuring time or keeping track of it. That's what separates the Internet from other time-consuming mediums. If you get mesmerized by TV over the course of an evening, the start of each new program reminds you that another hour has passed, and Jay Leno's monologue lets you know it's almost midnight. Unlike a magazine with its concise table of contents and finite number of articles, the Internet offers no organization for its limitless sources of information and entertainment. Even the most gripping suspense novel that may keep you awake until the early morning hours does have an ending. If you couldn't put it down while you were reading it, at least you stop when it's finished and note the passage of time. But the Internet is a *War and Peace* with thousands more pages and no ending—just endless chapters, innumerable plot twists, and characters that continue to come and go for as long as you choose to stick with them.

## DROPPING BY FOR A "BRIEF" CHAT

A typical Internet user may find it easy to let a few hours slide by while surfing the Web for information. But for most users, that's usually more inconvenient than addictive or destructive. Time gets chewed up faster and more frequently in the newsgroups, chat rooms, and interactive games. That's where the user becomes more directly engaged with what's happening on-line.

Rather than passively reading information or looking at the Web's colorful graphics, chat room or interactive game users get actively involved in two-way communication with other users—and lots of them. Some chat rooms gather more than 1,000 users in a single room, so going inside can be more stimulating than frequenting a popular bar. And as at a bar, the action in a chat room tends to pick up later at night when more regulars have finished dinner and chores and settled into their computer stations. Unlike bars, however, chat rooms have no closing hour. So people like Robin, whom we visited at the opening of this chapter, can hang out all through the night.

Raymond, a sales manager in a department store in Vancouver, British Columbia, began using the Internet strictly for information. But he vividly recalls when he first stumbled into a chat room. "That day I first pressed People Connection, my whole life changed!" he relates. "I went from using the Internet an hour a day to 10 hours a day. My daily routine is to get up early just to read my e-mail before I go to work, to see which friends I've met in the chat rooms have left me messages. As soon as I get home, I turn the computer back on. I stay up to 1 A.M. and have to force myself to get off. But on the weekend, I am on literally from the moment I wake up to the moment I go to bed. I just can't spend enough time on it."

Many chat rooms have specific themes. As a golfer, Raymond first gravitated toward Golfers Chat. Jerry, an accountant and avid skier who frequents the slopes near his home in Utah, chose to hang out in SkiBums. Or you may just go room-hopping to sample several different groups with diverse clienteles. In any chat room, you might find yourself arguing, debating, brainstorming, gossiping, feuding, flirting, falling in love—or just chatting. Dialogue flows rapidly and haphazardly. Anyone can type a message at any time, and each message appears in the scrolling text in the order entered. You can direct your comment to the entire group or to just one person, but everyone still sees your message in the ongoing chat flow that scrolls down your screen. In pinball-like fashion, comments bounce across the room from all corners.

Here's a typical conversation shared by one of the people in my study, who used the name (or handle) Midnight Cowboy. I've left the shorthand popular among chat rooms intact, along with notations such as <s> for smile, *lol* for laughing out loud, and extra punctuation marks such as {{{ for emphasis or attention. This conversation unfolded at 10 A.M. on a Saturday:

MIDNIGHT COWBOY: *Hey, I just woke up.*

CALIF GUY: *You probably need some coffee.*

NICOLE: *So, u in ur jameys or don't u wear anything to bed?*

THE MECHANIC: *lol*

MIDNIGHT COWBOY: *{{{ boxers, actually }}}*

NICOLE: *mmm, what color?*

CALIF GUY: *I guess u don't need any coffee, just a good rub-down from Nicole.*

LUVNKISSES: *{{{{ Good morning all }}}*

MIDNIGHT COWBOY: *White with little red hearts, do u like?*

THE MECHANIC: *Hi luv, how r u?*

NICOLE: *Yes, they sound lovely ;-)*

LUVNKISSES: *Good, but having a rough morning.*

MIDNIGHT COWBOY: *I don't have much on besides my boxers, how about u?*

THE MECHANIC: *Let me give you a nice warm cup of coffee--cream or sugar?*

LUVNKISSES: *Just cream.*

NICOLE: *Bunny feet jameys, is that sexy or what . . . lol*

THE MECHANIC: *Here u go <s>*

LUVNKISSES: *Thanks, my luv to you :-) you are so kind!*

THE MECHANIC: *I aim to please <S>, so is it warm enough?*

LUVNKISSES: *Just right <wink>*

CALIF GUY: *Hey, would you like a blueberry muffin with that, luv?*

LUVNKISSES: *mmm, a warm muffin sounds great with my coffee . . . did you make it yourself?*

CALIF GUY: *Well, I do bake and these are warming by the window.*

As Midnight Cowboy and Nicole flirt, other characters exchange greetings and comments of their own in this jumbled conversation that took less than a minute to spill across the screen. You need to pay close attention to keep up with what's said and find your place to jump in. Obviously, the conversation is not a scintillating display of exciting ideas and provocative opinions, but chat room regulars say it's just this sort of mundane gabbing about the everyday matters of life that puts them into a hypnotic trance.

Janice, a 28-year-old management consultant from Ohio, lives mostly out of a suitcase. She hops planes for a new destination several times per week, and when she does come home it's often on the red-eye. She hasn't much time for a social life, so the chat rooms fill a void. Sometimes she's so tired and talked out from work, she doesn't even type a single comment of cyberchat herself. But she lurks for hour upon hour anyway.

"I just watch the text scroll up on the screen," explains Janice. "It's better than watching the fake characters you see on TV shows. At least these folks are real people, and I feel part of the conversation with them even if I don't engage in it."

During my study, I occasionally visited the Meeting Place, an on-line equivalent to a singles bar, to learn more about what goes on there. I remember clicking on one evening after dinner, intending to chat with a few people for an hour or so. I discussed the pros and cons of cold winters with a man from Florida. A woman from Colorado confided in me about her divorce, though she had no idea I was a psychologist. A British gentleman and I shared opinions about our favorite movies. When I finally glanced at my watch, it was well past midnight. Where did the time go? More important, what are we missing when we slip into the Terminal Time Warp?

## THE HUMAN COST OF LOST TIME

As Internet users continue to invest more time on longer on-line sessions, they naturally begin to devote less time and attention to other activities and people in their life. Sam, a Manhattan marketing executive, used to walk to his corner store every Sunday morning to pick up the Sunday papers and a couple of magazines. Now, he says, "I just sit in my pj's and click on *The New York Times*." He no longer catches the early morning summer breeze or the first view of a sunny sky. He misses those opportunities to bump into an old friend or engage in small talk with the store clerk he's known for 15 years.

Jerry, the skier in Utah, has not gone near the slopes all winter. He now spends his entire winter weekend days on the Internet. No more exhilarating downhill runs, no more warm conversations by the fire with old and new friends.

Howard used to go bowling every Wednesday night with the guys from his auto manufacturing plant in Michigan. But after his first month with America Online, he stayed in on Wednesday night—and every other evening—so he could scan the chat rooms looking for women who might want to flirt or even engage in cybersex. "I think that's better than bowling," Howard chuckles. But he's missing out on socializing with his buddies and the exercise he got from bowling.

When the Internet beckons you with newfound pleasure and wonder, it often replaces every other hobby or social activity. It becomes the focal point of your life, and your on-line sessions grow longer and more intense. You forget to eat dinner, pick up the kids at school, feed the dog, or get to the grocery store before it closes. If you have chores or duties you don't want to do, the Internet becomes a handy excuse to put them off.

"I know I have to get my laundry, food shopping, and stuff like that done during the day," admits Renee, a 25-year-old homemaker. "But when I'm on the Internet I find myself saying 'later, later' about those other things. I stopped taking my daily walks and exercising the way I used to. Sometimes I'm still in my robe at 3 in the afternoon, or I simply forget to eat lunch. And I still haven't called the plumber to fix the pipe in the bathroom that's been broken for three weeks. I keep saying to myself, 'Well, I'll get to that tomorrow for sure.' But tomorrow is the same story."

For Raymond, the Internet allowed him to talk about his golf game endlessly. But when his real-life golf buddies called him for their Sunday morning rounds at the local golf club, Raymond told them he had to stay home to work on his kitchen remodeling project. Truth is, that project also had been on hold for months because of his Internet obsession. The floors were strewn with plasterboard, and electrical wires dangled from torn-out light fixtures. Raymond's wife declared the room off-limits to their two daughters, ages six and four, and her dinner menu was limited to takeout and microwave leftovers. "Whenever the subject comes up with my wife," he says, "it causes huge fights between us."

The kitchen is not all that's gone neglected in Raymond's house while he immerses himself in People Connection. He also has tuned out his daughters. When he bought the computer, he had imagined learning it as a family project—a cozy scene of initial Internet lessons to the girls as they became old enough to go on-line. But as his own Internet fascination rapidly evolved into absorption and then obsession, he became less and less willing to share it. And because he now runs directly to the Internet when he comes home after his store closes in late evening, he hardly sees his children at all.

"I don't even help them with their homework in the evening because I'm in the chat rooms, and I don't help put them to bed because I don't realize how late it is," he confides. "I also don't help them get ready for school in the morning like I used to do, because I'm checking my e-mail. And I just can't stop myself."

Raymond's confessions were echoed in my survey by Internet addicts from all over the world. Spending time with loved ones and keeping up with daily chores rank at the top of the list of what gets lost as users get hooked on the Internet. Here's a Top 10 list of the most commonly mentioned activities that suffered because of excessive Internet use:

1. Time with partner or family.
2. Daily chores.
3. Sleep.
4. Reading.
5. Watching TV.
6. Time with friends.
7. Exercise.
8. Hobbies (gardening, woodworking, sewing).
9. Sex.
10. Social events (movies, plays, concerts).

You may recognize that many of these activities have been getting short shrift in your own life. If you came up with a high score in the Internet Addiction Test in Chapter 1, you know that you're not giving some people and activities the same energy and attention you used to give them. As you've become more connected with your computer, you've begun to lose connections with what's around you. Understanding this truth can be a first step toward changing it.

## RECOVERY STRATEGY 1:

### *Recognize What You're Missing*

Take your own inventory of what you've cut down on, or cut out, because of the time you're spending on the Internet. You may use my Top 10 list as a starting point, but look into your own habits and passions to make sure you include a full assessment. Perhaps you're spending less time hiking, golfing, fishing, or camping. Maybe you have stopped going to ball games, or visiting the zoo, or volunteering at church. Have you been turning down every invitation to parties? Do you travel less? Have you kept your boat in dry dock all year?

Write down every activity or practice you've neglected or curtailed since your Internet habit emerged. Now rank each one on this scale of 1 to 3:

1—Very Important
2—Important
3—Not Very Important

In rating your lost activities, genuinely try to remember your life before the Net. How did you regard each endeavor then? Have your feelings about them really changed? Then look at what you labeled Very Important. Consider for a moment just what you are missing by giving up this activity. Didn't it once improve the quality of your life? Have you really meant to allow it to fall by the wayside? As your Internet time has risen and your time with other activities has dropped, you've been making choices. But it's possible that you've been making them unconsciously. This exercise will help you become more aware of the choices you make regarding the Internet and open the door to new decisions.

For each activity on your list, carefully consider which matters more: the Internet or the lost activity. Be sure to give full weight to the impact of what you're missing. You may find yourself initially dismissing the significance of a little lost sleep, often the first casualty of increased on-line time. But look further. Note the degree to which you may be relying on stimulants like coffee and caffeine-laden soft drinks to keep you awake later and later, more and more frequently. Some Internet addicts admit to taking caffeine pills to keep them clicking away at odd hours of the night. What harm are you doing to your body with such practices, and what long-term consequences might you be unwittingly inviting? And in the short term, do you really want to feel drowsy and fuzzy-headed during your workday?

Logging off the Internet at a reasonable hour requires discipline and control for most Internet users, even when you *do* know what time it is. Too many temptations lurk inside the on-line world you've come to depend on. As we mentioned, many chat rooms don't really get lively until late at night. And befriending someone in a different time zone adds a new complication. Many Internet addicts in the East stay up until midnight because that's the hour (9 P.M. Pacific time) their California cyber-friend gets home from work and gets on-line. On the other side of the sleep deprivation chart, exchanging messages in real time with a friend in England often means staying up until 3 A.M. With the five-hour time difference it's 8 A.M. for your friend, who may be getting up early on his end to block off some time before work to chat with *you!*

Such sleep-depriving routines inevitably take their toll. To combat the overriding fatigue and maintain their on-line habit, many users turn to a sleep/wake cycle: Use the Internet for a few hours; sleep for a few hours; go back on for a few hours; sleep for a few more hours. This is a popular rhythm among college students, especially those with Internet access in their own dorm room. Also, people who are unemployed or housebound find that without a structure to their days and nights, they can spend most of their time on-line with occasional breaks for sleep when their eyes grow weary or their back gets sore.

Losing sleep still may be primarily an individual consideration, but when Internet usage creeps into what had been shared time with your partner or your family, you are damaging your relationships. Your partner or child misses your presence and attention. They get jealous toward your growing affection with the Internet. They ask: "What can you be doing on the computer all that time?" They criticize you for immersing yourself so completely that you appear to lose track of time. Arguments begin. Distrust builds. You may find yourself slipping into patterns of secrecy and lies, or covering up your on-line time and behavior—all major signs of addiction.

## THE "ONE MORE MINUTE" SYNDROME

Tom has a wife and three kids who relied on him for company, conversation, and family activities before he discovered the Internet. Now they can't even walk into his computer room to ask him a simple question without encountering his hostility. "I'm so irritated that I tell my wife to get out of the room," Tom relates. "Then my kids will wander in to see where Dad is. I get so frustrated that I yell at them, too. It's like I'm on a high that I don't want to come down from. When they bother me, my high is broken."

After a few arguments like Tom's, you may innocently fall into what I call the "one more minute" syndrome. When someone in your life interrupts you or asks when you'll get off the computer so they can talk to you, instead of snapping at them and triggering a fight you may calmly say: "I'll be there in just one more minute." You might actually believe it yourself.

But 10 minutes later, you're still calling up Web sites, answering the latest e-mail from your newsgroups, or following the action in a chat room. An hour later, you're so caught in the Terminal Time Warp that it still seems like a minute or two since you were first interrupted. Then your partner comes in for a second attempt to drag you away, and again you say: "I'll be there in just one more minute!" Only this time, there's more anger and resentment behind your message. Like Tom, you're protecting your "high" and you may perceive your intruder as bugging you every two minutes, when in fact it's been two hours.

This Internet experience can be compared to the response of an alcoholic who says to a loved one (or himself) "just one more drink" at a party, or the smoker who tells herself "just one more cigarette" before going to bed, or the gambler who assures his companion that he'll leave the casino after "just one more bet." You may know that you should be answering the call of your loved one to log off, or it's well past a reasonable hour to go to bed, or there's something else you really need to be doing, but you rationalize that "one more minute" won't make much difference.

But if you're not counting the hours you spend online, your partner and family certainly are. They see your habits change. They observe you staggering to the computer first thing in the morning to check your e-mail. They watch you rush to the terminal as soon as you get home from work or school. They notice when your two hours per night expands to three hours, then six hours. They feel the difference in your relationship when your routine shifts from using the Internet every other night to every night, and from one weekend morning to full days on both Saturday and Sunday. After several "one more minute" deflections that turned into hours, they decide they need to take more direct and dramatic action to get your attention.

Many frustrated family members who have contacted me told me they tried to force the addict in their lives to cut down or curtail Internet usage. That usually doesn't work. When Cheryl's husband had reached his limit of hearing Cheryl say "one more minute" as she cloistered herself in the chat rooms, he took the computer away from her. Cheryl countered with her own direct move.

"First I pleaded with him to give it back to me, but that was no use," Cheryl remembers. "But I wasn't going to let him stop me from using the Internet, so I called up a girlfriend and she let me use her on-line account. Then I started spending more and more time at her house. My husband was so upset that I was never home that he actually gave me the computer back. One way or another, I was going to get to the Internet."

The parents of 15-year-old Sheila tried to impose limits on her usage, just as parents often restrict their children's TV-watching hours. The new rule: two hours on-line per night, and not until homework is completed. At first, Sheila pleaded with them to allow her an hour or two more each night. They didn't give in, and because her computer was in her bedroom, she found that she could just bypass their limits. "After a while, I just didn't care what my parents thought so I just ignored their rules," she asserts. "I felt like they were taking away something good in my life, something I enjoy."

Partners and family members who confront an Internet addict usually point first to the time the user devotes to this new love. But when the addict hardly notices the true passage of time while on-line, she or he may deny the full scope of the problem, saying: "Oh, I can't be spending 50 hours a week on the Internet. Seems more like 15 or 20." The confronting family member feels invalidated and may snap back: "No, I'm sure it's at least 50 hours, and maybe it's even 75!" And the same arguments go back and forth, time and time again. If these confrontations have hit your home, consider a new approach.

## RECOVERY STRATEGY 2:

### Assess Your On-line Time

To get a clear idea of how much time you (or the Internet addict in your life) spend on this habit, it helps to chart the actual number of hours involved. To get started, break down the categories of on-line activity that you favor and to what degree. Use the following checklist to determine where your Internet time goes. You may find that you can estimate your total number of hours spent per week on each Internet application to gain a fair assessment of your overall investment, especially if you ask for input from a loved one with a better sense of reality. Or if you aim for greater accuracy, you may choose to keep an actual time log for a typical week on the Internet.

1. *Chat rooms.* How many hours spent per week? List all the different chat rooms you visit.
2. *Interactive games.* How many hours? Name the different games you play.
3. *E-mail.* How many hours? Track how many e-mail messages you send and receive each day.
4. *Newsgroups.* How many hours? List the different groups you participate in.
5. *World Wide Web.* How many hours? Identify your favorite Web site subjects.

6. *Other Internet usage.* Are there additional applications you've discovered on the Internet? Name them and similarly total your hours spent per week on each one.

Compare the time spent on each application and rank the order of your favorite usages. Now you have a detailed assessment of the on-line hangouts you prefer and how much time they drain from your everyday life. Add all the hours you devote in each category to determine your total hours consumed by the Internet. Surprised? You're not alone. Most Internet users in my study told me they were amazed to discover the full scope of their on-line devotion. Then they'd ask me what it meant. In other words, how much time makes an addiction?

## How Much Is Too Much?

There's no arbitrary cutoff that separates normal or acceptable Internet use from an addictive habit. You can't define any addiction by quantity alone. Instead, the problems the habit causes in your life rate as a more accurate addiction barometer, as you learned in taking the Internet Addiction Test in Chapter 1. With alcohol, you can't arbitrarily say that 10 beers is okay but 11 or more tilts the glass toward addiction. Similarly, I can't tell you that 10 hours per week is fine, but when you slip into that 11th hour you've become an Internet addict.

Respondents to my survey told me they stayed on-line 4, 5, or even 10 hours a day during the week, then shot up to 10 to 14 hours a day on the weekend—every week. That's 40 to 78 hours per week of Internet time *not* performing mandatory tasks for work or school. Rather, this represents time spent with no business or academically related purpose—just surfing or chatting. The average weekly usage of those who fit the criteria of Internet addiction was *38 hours.*

When you reach that degree of usage, you most likely have fallen into a habit that leads to the sort of real-time problems that constitute addictive behavior: the craving, the concealing, the lying. You turn to the Internet for emotional support. You use it as a substitute for what is missing in your real life. You create an on-line fantasy world that's more fulfilling than your own. You act different toward others when you're around the computer. You think about the Internet when you're not on-line, and when you want to avoid disturbing questions about yourself. And your dependence grows.

When Internet addicts explain their rapid progression of hours invested on-line, they sound like someone hooked on a physical substance. Robin, the once-disciplined woman whom we saw staying up all night with the Internet at the start of this chapter, says that when she's on-line she feels like "I'm taking some drug, and I just can't stop taking more of it." John, a construction worker who maintains a 50-hour habit with the aid of caffeine pills, also describes a druglike experience. "I wish I could just inject more of this stuff right into my veins!" he confesses.

A lighthearted exaggeration? Perhaps, but the escalating hours of Internet usage do clearly illustrate a growing tolerance for the practice, just as an alcoholic develops a greater tolerance for alcohol. As the user, you need more of the substance or practice to achieve the same desired effect; the "high" you first got from half an hour in a chat room may take you two hours to duplicate. This breeds dependence.

It also makes any attempt to turn back the clock on time spent on the Internet all the more difficult. I asked Internet users: "Have you ever tried to cut down your net usage and failed?" Eighty-two percent answered yes. So it's common to lose control over your Internet usage.

THE TERMINAL TIME WARP    55

Like smokers who say they can quit at any time, those who try to stop using the Internet find that actually doing it becomes a tortuous endeavor.

Kim is a college student who maintained a 3.5 grade point average when she began partying in the Internet chat rooms. She didn't worry about the lost sleep and missed classes at first. "I can quit if I really have to," she would tell her mother and her friends. When her average dipped to a 1.8, she decided it was time to stop—and she couldn't. "After three days off-line, I couldn't stop thinking about all my Net friends," she admits. "I couldn't concentrate on reading, studying for tests, doing homework. I felt terrible, just like a smoker who has gone all day without smoking. I needed my Internet fix. That's when I knew I had a problem. I learned how powerful this addiction is and that I needed help with it."

You don't need to be hooked completely on the Net to discover that stopping, or even cutting down, requires all the assistance you can muster. People who find themselves suddenly spending a little more time on-line than they really wanted to, or meant to, soon understand that willpower or discipline alone seldom will reverse the pattern. Many Internet addicts I interviewed insisted that they had sincerely tried to cut down their time and curb the problems caused by their excessive use. But in talking to them, I found that they had sabotaged their efforts with basic mistakes.

Some tried to quit cold turkey, but they failed to anticipate the real withdrawal symptoms that would follow, or they lacked the resources to develop healthy, positive alternatives to gain what the Internet was supplying in their lives. Like Kim, they crawled back to the computer within a few days of stopping. Others made efforts to cut down their time invested a little here and a little there, but they didn't set up a structure that would help keep them on course.

I believe that moderation of Internet use is possible. You don't have to give up the Internet entirely to recover from an addiction to it, unlike addictions to substances that require total abstinence. But in attempting to regain control over the time you spend, it helps to follow specific guidelines.

## RECOVERY STRATEGY 3:
### *Use Time-Management Techniques*

You can begin to manage your on-line time in several ways. I'll outline four different routes to pursue. You may find you like one or that a combination of two, three, or all four provides you the most solid means to better control. As you read each approach, decide what might work best for you, but be open to changing your mind as needed. Experimenting is encouraged.

1. *Cultivate an alternative activity.* If you think of a hobby you always wanted to try, this could be the most opportune time to begin it. If you have talked about joining the local fitness center, do it now. Perhaps you remember an old friend you haven't talked to in a long time; reach out to that person now and see what you might want to do together. Make it something you will enjoy. The more fun things you do in your life every day, the less you will miss that constant Internet buzz and give in to the craving to go back to it.

2. *Identify your usage pattern and practice the opposite.* Take a few moments to consider your current habits of using the Internet. What days of the week do you typically log online? What time of day do you usually begin? How long do you stay on during a typical session? Where do you usually use the computer?

To begin to shake the habit, practice the opposite. Let's say your Internet habit involves checking your e-mail first thing in the morning. Try hopping in the shower and starting breakfast first instead. If you only use the Internet at night, when you push on well beyond bedtime, use it only in the daytime now. If you turn to the computer before dinner, wait until after eating to go on-line. If you use it every weeknight, wait until the weekend, and if you're an all-weekend user, shift to just weeknights. If you never take breaks, take one at least every half hour. If your usage started by calling up the newspaper on the Net, read the newspaper in print instead. If you use the computer in the den, move it to the bedroom.

This approach worked for Blaine, whose main problem had been staying on-line so long in the morning he would arrive hours late for work. Now he skips his morning on-line session and waits until evening to log on. "It was hard to change at first, almost like giving up my coffee in the morning," he relates. "But after a few days of struggling not to turn on the computer in the morning, I managed to get the hang of it. Now that I wait until evening to read my e-mail from friends, I get to work on time."

3. *Find external stoppers.* Use the concrete things you need to do and places you need to go as prompters to remind you when to log off the Internet, and schedule your time on-line just before them. If you should leave for work at 7:30 A.M., go on the Internet at 6:30 A.M. and tell yourself you have exactly one hour before it's time to quit. Or let's say you have a ceramics class at 8 P.M. on Tuesday. Log on at 6:30 P.M. that night and stay on until it's time to leave for class. If you're meeting a friend for lunch at 12:30 P.M. on Saturday, allow yourself to go on-line at 10:30 A.M. for two hours before your appointment. Or de-

cide that you will begin to make dinner at 6:30 P.M., so sit down for an hour of usage at 5:30. You might also try to begin your on-line session an hour before your wife is to come home with the intention of stopping when she arrives, or logging on an hour before it's time to go to your child's school play.

The danger, of course, is that you'll ignore such natural alarms. If so, try a real alarm clock. Determine the time you will end a session and set an alarm on your watch, an alarm clock, an egg timer, or anything that makes noise. Keep it a few steps from the computer so you have to get up to shut it off.

4. *Incorporate planned Internet time into your weekly schedule.* Many attempts to limit Internet usage fail because the user relies on an ambiguous plan to trim hours without determining when those remaining on-line slots will come. I suggest a different approach. Set a reasonable goal, perhaps 20 hours a week on-line instead of your current 40. Then schedule those 20 hours in specific time slots and write them on your calendar or weekly planner. Keep the sessions brief and frequent. This will help you avoid cravings and withdrawal, and regular two-hour sessions will steer you away from falling into the time warp.

As an example of a 20-hour schedule, you might plan on using the Internet from 8 to 10 P.M. every weeknight, and 1 to 6 P.M. on Saturday and Sunday. Or a new 10-hour schedule might include two weeknight sessions from 7:30 to 10:30 P.M., and an 8:30 A.M. to 12:30 P.M. treat on Saturday. Or you might try brief, daily sessions prescribed as a reward at the end of a tough day.

"One day at a time" is a recurring theme of 12-step recovery programs for alcoholism or drug addiction. Their goal is abstinence. For Internet dependency a relevant motto might be "one time a day," meaning you need to limit your Internet usage to one short, specific period each day or on your prescribed schedule of days. Incorporating a tangible schedule of Internet use will give you a sense of being in control, rather than having the Internet control you.

## A WORD OF CAUTION

For many Internet users, these time-management techniques may not necessarily work on the first or second attempt. It's not an instant cure for what may have become a major problem, and the user trying to regain control must be motivated to begin and to stick with it. For someone who's really hooked, a deeper understanding of the underlying roots of their addiction and how it relates to their psychological and emotional needs may help fuel that motivation. I'll be addressing those roots in the following chapter, and I'll offer additional tools for specific problem areas.

For other Internet addicts, seeing the broader context of where their addiction most damages their life can serve as a trigger to seek change. In Chapters 5 to 8, we'll focus on the specific issues related to problems in relationships, family, school, and work. I'll offer specific recovery strategies that best fit each environment.

If, however, you had a relatively low score on the Internet Addiction Test in Chapter 1, time-management tools may be all you need to redirect your energy. And for any Internet user, assessing time spent on the Internet and practicing time-management techniques mark an important start toward a life where you use the Internet without getting addicted to it. This is an excellent time to begin.

# THREE

# Profiles of On-lineaholics

*I'm terrified of giving it up. I think I would be suicidal without it.*—COLLEGE SOPHOMORE ADDICTED TO MUDs

Not all Internet users get addicted to it. At home, work, and school, millions of people every day routinely send e-mail, research academic papers and business ideas, keep updated on the latest news, and enjoy colorful graphics and images from all over the world. These Internet users are not staying up all night in chat rooms or slaying dragons in interactive games. They are fully engaged in their real-life relationships. They still go to movies and plays, read books, take hikes in the woods, and keep up with daily chores and responsibilities. They can click off the Net when it's time to go to bed or get back to work.

And yet, every day rising numbers of Internet users or their loved ones come forward with distressing accounts of lives gone out of control. For them the simple act of entering their password has become the gateway to serious trouble. They have come to see the Internet not as a technological tool but as a technological temptation. Why have these Internet addicts been tossed into turmoil by the same piece of technology that others have integrated gracefully into balanced lives? Who's getting addicted today? Who's most at risk of becoming addicted tomorrow?

At this relatively early stage in the long-term evolution of the Internet, it is too early to draw grand conclusions. But as I've studied the habits and personalities of Internet addicts, I've begun to see the emergence of a profile of an *on-lineaholic.* Let's look at some case studies that typify the basic features of that profile. You may see yourself—or the Internet user you live with—in one or more of them. The insights we uncover about their lives will help you understand more about your own problems, and the suggested intervention strategies I outline will point you toward healthy and productive changes. You'll also learn tools that will help you to recognize the voices of denial.

To begin, let's examine some common assumptions and beliefs about who gets addicted to the Internet and why. Mental health professionals, the media, and Internet users themselves offer various theories about this new psychological dependency. Sometimes they've been right on target, but just as often I believe they've been operating under false assumptions that distort their perspective. Following are several of the most frequently mentioned beliefs, with my conclusions as to which are true, which are false, and why.

## Who Gets Addicted: A Reality Check

1. **Many Internet addicts suffer from significant emotional or psychiatric problems before they ever go online.**

*True.* In the survey, 54 percent of Internet addicts reported a prior history of depression. Another 34 percent suffered from anxiety, and others displayed chronically low self-esteem. Many of these respondents indicated that they were undergoing professional treatment for their problems, with several of them on medication. For such

Internet users who already are grappling with major problems in relationships, work, money, or school, their on-line addiction intensifies those struggles and brings on new complications.

## 2. Many Internet addicts are former alcoholics or other ex-addicts.

*True.* Fifty-two percent of my survey respondents admitted that they were following recovery programs for alcoholism, chemical dependency, compulsive gambling, or chronic overeating. In their approach to the Internet, these on-lineaholics could see the same excessive behavior, the same need for a crutch to help them relax, that they had exhibited in their prior addictions. Though they believe Internet addiction is not as serious as alcoholism, they still feel disheartened that a new addiction has substituted for the old.

## 3. Despite those reports of bored housewives getting hooked, the young, male computer-savvy "techie" is the prototype Internet addict.

*False.* Women comprised 61 percent of respondents to my survey. Although women may be more likely than men to participate in a study like this, it's clear that the old computer-nerd stereotype does not fit the Internet world. As for age, Pauline, a retired nurse with two grandsons, told me she never had touched a computer until joining the chat-room movement a year and a half ago. Finding herself on-line morning, noon, and night, she concludes that at age 64: "I need to get a life."

## 4. Male and female Internet addicts use the on-line world exactly the same way.

*False.* A high degree of stereotypical gender differences surfaced in the survey. Men generally appeared to be seeking power, status, and dominance. They gravitated more toward the sources of information glut, aggressive interactive games, and sexually explicit chat and cyberporn. Women embraced the chat rooms as a means to form supportive friendships, seek romance, or complain about their husbands. Women also enjoyed the comforting realization that no one they encountered on-line could know what they looked like.

5. **Many Internet addicts adopt new personas on-line.**

*True.* The idea of becoming someone different from whom they are lures many users into excessive Internet use. Some addicts go by several different "handles," changing their on-line persona according to their moods or desires. Others settle on one identity, either an ideal self that reflects the opposite of their everyday personality or a character that accesses a repressed emotion. With such rampant role playing, newbies must be aware that Internet characters are often not who or what they seem to be.

6. **Only introverts get hooked on the Internet's interactive applications.**

*False.* Nearly eighty percent of all on-lineaholics are primarily drawn to the two-way communication forums of chat rooms and interactive games, but they're not all shy. I asked Internet addicts in the survey how they'd describe their basic personality. Four of the top six responses were *bold, outgoing, open-minded,* and *assertive.* So while many users do flock to the chat rooms because they don't have anyone to talk to, as we'll see in more detail in the next chapter, many others go there just because they like to talk.

7. **Once confronted about their dependent behavior, Internet addicts generally will admit they have a problem and try to do something about it.**

*False.* Denial runs deep among Internet addicts, as it does with any addiction. But it's even more difficult to recognize and seek help for something that most people praise for its power and innovation or, at worst, shrug off as a harmless communication device. So even when presented with the clear evidence of addictive behavior, Internet addicts cocoon themselves in the cultural voice that says "the Internet is great" and try to wriggle free of admission and assistance. Those who contact me today are usually the loved ones of Internet addicts. They see the denial.

## A SINGLE MOM'S SPIRALING DEPRESSION

Wendy never has been happy living in San Diego. A small-town girl from Wisconsin, she moved to California several years ago when her husband was transferred there. When they divorced after several rounds of his violent, alcoholic behavior, Wendy yearned to move back to Wisconsin to be close to her parents. But with joint custody of the couple's 12-year-old son, Grant, she decided to stay in San Diego rather than subject him to long shuttles between parents.

Wendy had a good job as an administrative assistant for an engineering firm, but money was tight. When she had to have a hysterectomy a couple of years ago, she felt hopeless about her future. Only 37, she grieved the fact that she could never have more children. To make matters worse, the men she was meeting seemed to have many of her ex-husband's bad traits. Her closest women friends appeared happily married with growing families. When she socialized with them, Wendy felt like a third wheel.

"Everything was a mess in my life," Wendy recalls. "After the hysterectomy, I felt like I was not really a woman. I saw myself as a total failure, and I never thought it would be like this. I wanted a big, happy family and love in my life."

She turned to a psychologist for help and was referred to a psychiatrist who prescribed an antidepressant. To keep up with her escalating medical bills for her physical and emotional problems, Wendy took a second job doing secretarial work in a doctor's office. Wanting to work from home as much as possible to be near her son, she bought a modem for her home computer. That opened the door to Internet chat rooms.

"Right away, I met a single mom who also had lived with an abusive, alcoholic husband. We became best friends," Wendy relates. "We talked for hours privately about our problems, and she helped show me around to a bunch of different chat rooms. All of a sudden, I was no longer the third wheel going out with couples. And when I was on-line, all my pressures and troubles seemed to go away. It was like being absorbed in a good movie that lasted a long time."

This "movie" soon got in the way of a quality home life. As she immersed herself in her computer screen, she became less involved in her son's schoolwork. Their regular excursions to real-life movies or the beach disappeared. Then came the bills for the long connections to Prodigy, forcing Wendy to use up her remaining savings. Those once-balanced meals for Grant were replaced by a steady diet of macaroni and cheese. Still, she couldn't turn away from her chat room lifeline. She asked her psychologist for understanding and guidance. "He laughed at me and told me to just turn the computer off," she sighs. "That drove a wedge into our relationship, and I felt even more alone."

Feeling more desperate, she turned to the Internet newsgroup *alt.depression.* After her son went to bed at night, she poured out her frustrations to Internet users suffering from depression triggered by their own life struggles. With her bedtime pushed back to 2 or 3 A.M., her work suffered. She feared she could get fired. And now her Visa bill had reached her $2,000 credit limit, so she no longer could charge her hefty Prodigy fees. Wendy called her mother in Wisconsin and convinced her to lend her credit card to Wendy to "help pay for clothes for Grant."

Lying to her mother made Wendy feel guilty, which plunged her into greater depression. She began to sense that her Internet use really was not offering her a lasting solution to her troubles. Rather, her habit had become a major part of the problem. After reading a news account of my study, she contacted me.

### RECOVERY STRATEGY 4:
## *Find Support in the Real World*

For Wendy, as with any Internet addict who suffers from depression, the first step in regaining control is to admit to the addiction. Then, to help break the dependence on the Internet, Wendy should identify the needs she was trying to fulfill on-line and seek to meet them in real life, with support from the people and resources around her.

To help her come to grips with her feelings about the abuse she suffered in her marriage, she might benefit from a battered wives group or support service. Group therapy also could provide Wendy an Internet-like forum of other people seeking validation and support for wrestling with life's problems. Only instead of just ruminating about them on a computer, these group members would be working toward making positive changes. To attract the same camaraderie she found from her on-line friends, Wendy might seek out groups of single mothers through a local church or social organization.

In the chat rooms, Wendy frequently found herself typing comments like, "I hate the world" or "I can't believe how unfair life is." When her chat friends echoed the same sense of anger and despair, they only encouraged her to retreat further from the world. She lacked motivation to change her life circumstances. Now she needs to step back into her real life and address her loneliness and alienation. To gain perspective on her own problems, she might try volunteer work with the elderly, ill, or disabled. To begin to reconnect with her lost zest for life, she could consider a new hobby like line dancing.

Wendy also needs to make amends with her family. By telling her mother the truth about the $2,000 loan, she risks blame and rejection, but if their relationship is strong and her mother understands that Wendy is actively seeking assistance for her problems, her mother may become an even stronger ally. Wendy also needs to reclaim quality time with her son—more movies and days at the beach. She also might use the Internet constructively with him to assist in his schoolwork, which would enable her to share something with him while reminding herself that the Internet does have valid uses.

In terms of her overall Internet usage, Wendy will benefit from the time-management techniques I outlined in Recovery Strategy 3 in the previous chapter. She should incorporate a limited number of Internet hours into her detailed weekly schedule. Eight hours per week might work best in her case. She may need an alarm clock to remind her when her on-line sessions have ended. With more energy and available time, she may even feel motivated to take a class or two at a local community college to advance her work skills and possibly move toward a new career. After all, she hasn't even reached age 40.

## The Legend of LambdaMOO

Steve never became the quarterback of his high school football team, as his father had hoped. He's not making the dean's list in his sophomore year at a major university in upstate New York, as his mother would like to see. She often reminds Steve that his older brother is pulling a solid 3.5 grade point average at Rutgers. Steve also has no friends at school and his girlfriend recently broke up with him.

But in LambdaMOO, all that changes. In Lambda-MOO, everyone bows to Steve in recognition of his power, skill, and intelligence. They respect and fear him. In LambdaMOO, Steve has buddies whom he can meet for drinks and small talk at Dred's Tavern. In Lambda-MOO, Steve charms every woman he meets. He's recently been dating the beautiful and charming SoftSnow. In LambdaMOO, Steve is regarded as a great wizard— the highest honor anyone can achieve.

LambdaMOO is the land of the Multi-User Dungeon (MUD) where Steve spends most of his time. MUD commonly refers to the Internet's many interactive games, including the pure adventure type and the more socially oriented games known as MUSHes and MOOs. Traditionally, a MUD is a spinoff of the old Dungeons and Dragons game, where players take on the names of characters who compete through fighting battles, buying weapons, engaging in duels, killing monsters, slaying dragons, storming castles, and saving maidens. There are hundreds of MUDs, each with its own theme. In *Star Trek,* you might find yourself captain of the Enterprise zapping away at Klingons. In Steve's LambdaMOO, 30 or more players simultaneously roam different chambers, alternately talking to a friend and ally, then fighting off an intruder.

As you win battles and duels, you gain cumulative points and rise in status. Steve's character, "Chameleon," has reached the level of wizard, the pinnacle of competing characters. That means all the other players must bow to him as an army private salutes a general. In the MUDs, wizards are immortal, just like the gods of Greek mythology. No one in the game can kill them, but they can destroy a newbie with one swift stroke of their virtual sword and then move in to pick up valuables from the virtual corpse.

Because MUDs never end—play is continuous day and night, week to week—the only way to become a wizard is to play often. Steve plays at least 60 to 70 hours every week, following a pattern of jumping on the computer immediately after dinner and staying with it until 2 or 3 A.M. Then he sleeps until noon, skipping his morning classes. He may attend an afternoon class or two before rushing back to his dorm for another night as Chameleon. His grades are slipping to basic passing level, but he hasn't seriously considered cutting down. He explains:

"MUDs are like religion to me, and I am a god there. I am respected by all the other MUDders. I know that I am playing against other highly intelligent people, and developing the winning strategies and getting stronger at the game gives me a great high. Even when I'm not playing, I'm wondering if there will be more newbies for me to kill that night or which other guys will be playing. I like having the power in my hands, to know that I am in control of my character and my destiny in this world. My character Chameleon is a legend, and I identify with him."

When he's not MUDding, Steve is held back by low self-esteem. He's shy and awkward around people and believes he doesn't fit in at school. He carries with him the critical voices of his parents, who remind him of his shortcomings. He doesn't feel comfortable around women on campus. He finds his classes boring. "My real life sucks, and my MUD life is great," Steve concludes. "When I'm playing the MUDs, I'm not feeling lonely or mopey. I'm not thinking about my problems. I just forget all that, and I want to stay on the MUDs as long as I possibly can."

But when Steve read a notice about my study on a bulletin board at school, he requested to meet with me. He recognized that as much as he reveled in his MUD achievements, the strains of his real life were becoming more overwhelming every day. He fought more with his parents, who caught on to his Internet habit, and now his roommate was on him for hogging the phone line most of the night with his modem. He couldn't concentrate on his studies because they just didn't compare with MUDs. His increased self-esteem in LambdaMOO didn't translate into better feelings about himself when the computer was off.

"I know I have an addiction to this, but I also know that I'm terrified of giving it up," he told me. "I think I would be suicidal without it."

### RECOVERY STRATEGY 5:
#### *Recognize Your Addictive Triggers*

For Steve, as with any Internet addict who goes on-line to avoid facing low self-esteem or other emotional problems, certain feelings usually trigger their on-line sessions. Consider your own feelings when you head toward the computer for another five hours on-line. Complete the following sentence: **Before I turn to the Internet, I feel _____.**

Are you worn out from work or worried about money? Do you wish you could avoid your responsibilities at home? Are you sad because you have so few friends and life seems boring? Steve said that he often felt sad, lonely, bored, or miserable before he went for his fix of MUDs. He would tell himself that he was no good, that nothing else he did mattered, that no one really cared about him. Others have reported feeling depressed, anxious, angry, or stressed. These are the feelings that prompt you to rush back to the Internet, and they're part of the drive of your addictive behavior.

Now think for a moment about how different every-thing looks when you go on-line. Complete this sentence: **When I am engaged in my favorite Internet activity, I feel** _____.

Do you feel relaxed, welcoming the Internet as an an-tidote to your anxiety? Or do you feel excited and happy, rather than bored and depressed as you were before your session began? For Steve, going on-line made him feel confident, competent, fulfilled, and respected. Other typical answers include calm, happy, excited, loved, sup-ported, sexy, happy, and hopeful.

Recognizing these two feeling states—how you feel before you go on-line and how you feel when you're us-ing the Net—allows you to see what you're running away from and tune in to what you hope to gain on-line. Each time you decide to use the Internet as a response to these triggers, you face a *choice point*.

When you hit this point, you can observe the emo-tional triggers and choose to turn to a more constructive activity, or you can give in to your pattern of excessive In-ternet use in hopes of chasing away the bad feelings and recapturing the pleasant ones.

When Steve reached his choice point, he usually re-jected the option of studying, going to bed, or socializing on campus in favor of enhancing his image in Lambda-MOO. At choice points, Internet addicts like Steve are dominated by negative messages that prompt them to say to themselves: "I have to turn on the computer now" or "I need to stay on as long as last night for it to be as good" or "I must check out who's on-line right now." Steve often found himself thinking: "MUDs are God to me. They are my home." Such messages can sabotage your best efforts at maintaining control of your usage.

With practice and determination, however, you can substitute positive messages that lead you toward health-ier goals. You can tell yourself: "I will quit at my regular bedtime so I won't skip class (or be late for work) tomorrow" or "I am in control of my life when I decide how and when to use the Internet."

Steve responded to these kinds of positive suggestions because they reminded him of how he achieves mastery in the MUDs, through a confident attitude and determination to stick with his goals. Using the time-management techniques I've outlined, he scheduled two hours of Internet use every night, from 10 P.M. to midnight. He studied for three hours after dinner, and he regarded his MUD session as a reward for his discipline. When midnight loomed and he feared losing his legend status because of his lesser commitment to the game, he told himself: "I'll get off the computer when I said I will." More and more, he was able to follow this new program.

With the help of additional counseling at college, Steve gradually regained control over his Internet usage and his life. He even found a new hobby—chess. Upon joining the school's chess club, he met new friends on campus. And when he won a match, he found his self-esteem rising in a way he used to experience only in LambdaMOO.

## BURIED EMOTIONS AWAKENED ON-LINE

In our initial tour of Internet addicts in Chapter 1 we met Tony, a recently married construction worker who each night transforms from mild-mannered husband to "aggressive bastard" when he plays the interactive game DOOM-II. Tony called me seeking help after reading about my research in *The Philadelphia Inquirer.*

Like many male Internet users who flood the interactive games, Tony threw himself fully into the fights and battles, the slayings of dragons and monsters. He enjoyed those aggressive feelings and played more and more often to experience them, but he began to feel the same destructive urges toward his wife. When she interrupted him during a game, he would snap: "Get out of here and leave me alone!" He also had an 18-month-old daughter, and the idea of turning his aggression loose at home terrified him. He always had considered himself to be calm and gentle, so he couldn't understand how such impulses could be stirred in him.

Tony is typical of the Internet user who accesses buried emotions on-line. Even before he began using the Internet, he had those feelings of anger and the ability to behave aggressively but didn't realize it. In our interview I helped him trace their origins. Growing up as a middle child, he often felt ignored by his parents and resentful of his siblings. But he stifled those feelings and lived up to his mother's ideal of the good little boy, all the way through the years he lived with his family as a single, working adult until marrying Faye at 32.

Faye didn't like Tony's male friends from work and directed him to stay home and work on the kitchen and family room instead of going out with the guys. He agreed. He also took on freelance carpentry work on weekends. Not surprisingly, he felt tied down at home and in his marriage. "I got married because I felt that was what you're supposed to do," he says. "And we had a kid because I thought that's what you're supposed to do."

With his wife, Tony was replaying the role of the good little boy, only now he was the good husband who always did what he was told and what was expected of him. He was building up anger about it, and DOOM-II had become the place where that anger spilled out. But now that he had unlocked his aggression, it was more difficult for him to suppress it again. And he lacked the tools and insights to channel it appropriately into his everyday life.

I urged Tony to find a therapist to help him process his anger toward his parents and siblings and recognize the connection between those early experiences and his current life situation. In time, he will learn to assert his basic needs in his marriage, to stand up for himself in an appropriate way and tell Faye what he really wants in their marriage. Couples counseling might help them both work out new agreements and make adjustments in their unconscious roles. Then, Tony's overwhelming need to spend five hours a night beating up imaginary opponents will begin to subside.

## A SUBSTITUTE ADDICTION

Ken, an attorney in the suburbs of New York, used to drink a case and a half of beer every week. He suffered blackouts and barely escaped major injury one night when he got drunk and wrecked his car. His wife, Vicki, told him repeatedly that he had a problem, but he didn't see it until the day of his father's funeral. "That's when it hit me—my father was an alcoholic and I had become one, too," Ken admits. "I started going to AA meetings the next day, and I've been sober ever since."

That was nearly two years ago. Because of Ken's long hours at work and in court, his AA sponsor suggested that he use the AA support group on the Internet between in-person meetings. That's where Ken encountered Helen, a recovering alcoholic with whom he found much in common. Helen invited him to a separate on-line room for a private conversation, then guided him into other Net hangouts, including the chat rooms. Ken's Internet time instantly shot up to seven or eight hours some days.

Vicki began monitoring his hours on-line just as she had monitored his drinking, and she got just as angry about it. She had been looking forward to the opportunity to enjoy the company of a sober husband and do more things together and with their two sons. Now a new addiction had invaded their home. Ken tried to listen to her, but he struggled to grasp how this new practice could be as damaging as his old addiction.

"I had the same kind of anticipation before going on-line that I had before drinking. When I was away from it, I really felt like I needed that fix again. And I was losing control over how much time I spent," Ken concedes. "But I wasn't having blackouts or car crashes, and I could rationalize that using the Internet all the time even kept me from drinking."

Still, the arguments with Vicki escalated, and his close friendship with Helen deepened. Like most on-lineaholics, Ken began to lie. Sometimes he and Vicki fought in front of his two boys, which especially distressed Ken. He sent me an e-mail requesting information about Internet addiction and guidance on what to do about it.

## A New Challenge for Recovery Communities

I reminded Ken that the first step in any recovery is to admit to the problem. He needed to understand that although the Internet is not a physical substance and doesn't harm the body, it's still a powerful addiction capable of doing real damage to his marriage, family, and potentially his work. But this admission can be especially challenging for any Internet user with a prior addiction. Even in recovery circles, addicts often get trapped into thinking in terms of a hierarchy of addictions: Drug addiction is worse than alcoholism; alcoholism is worse than nicotine addiction; nicotine addiction is worse than chronic overeating, and so on. So some addictive behavior gets overlooked or at least put on hold while the person in recovery focuses on steering clear of the "more serious" addiction.

With such hierarchical thinking, Internet addiction gets placed on the bottom rung of the ladder. As Ken said, no blackouts and no car wrecks had occurred, so he had a safe addiction. But he still was continuing his pattern of addictive behavior—excessive usage, losing control, arguing, avoiding problems. I urged Ken to discuss this issue with his AA sponsor, who should recognize and understand how Ken's new addiction was undermining his general recovery. Sharing his Internet experiences at an open AA meeting, however, could be risky; he might find validation and support for his willingness to confront this new obsession, but he might just as easily be dismissed for getting sidetracked from what others perceived as his main goal. They might tell him not to worry about the computer and to direct all his energy toward staying sober. I told Ken that if he didn't gain solid support for dealing with Internet addiction in his recovery community, it was critical that he find an addiction counselor or therapist who would take it seriously.

In therapy, Ken likely would learn that he was using the Internet to avoid facing the same life problems that his drinking had masked. Despite success at work, Ken was failing in his marriage and family. He wasn't emotionally available to Vicki, and he admitted that he had never been there for his two sons during his drinking days or now in his Internet obsession.

Ken would benefit from finding the roots of his low self-esteem, insecurity, and fear of intimacy. Learning new communication tools would help him open to his feelings with his wife and express them appropriately. And as part of his recovery from Internet addiction, I would recommend that Ken give up all usages except for an occasional AA on-line group with no private chats on the side. Instead, he might look to cultivate supportive friendships from his real-life circle of fellow recovering alcoholics.

## A Tranquilizer on a Keyboard

Susan, whom we met briefly in Chapter 1 as she lamented the ending of an on-line friendship, has always been the anxious type. She used to get anxious about her job as a financial analyst, and after she got laid off six months ago, she got even more anxious about the new house and new car she had bought with the expectation of a professional salary. She gets anxious about her marriage. At 38, she's living with her second husband, Richard, after an early divorce, and this new relationship also has its problems, especially because Richard's job as a reporter keeps him out late most nights. Susan is also anxious about living in Detroit. She's anxious about how people look at her and what they think about how she acts and the way she lives her life. She always believed most of her women coworkers judged her as inferior because she wasn't as aggressive or ambitious as them.

Susan is quick to grab for something to calm her nerves or relieve her upset stomach. She smokes almost constantly, takes antiacids, and while in therapy she recently was given an antianxiety medication. But home alone and out of work, Susan stumbled on a form of medication that appeared to work better than all the rest: the Internet chat rooms. She chatted about the weather and the different climates of various users from all over the world. She chatted about money and investments. She chatted about children, which she still hoped to have someday. She chatted about movies and TV shows and who was dating whom within the on-line communities she favored. She felt good—she only reached for a cigarette every half hour or so.

"I wasn't nervous or tense, just so relaxed," Susan remembers. "I would forget all my problems. And the people I met there really seemed to like me."

Always a people pleaser, Susan found her real-life friends much harder to satisfy. With her high-powered coworkers, she never knew what kind of birthday or Christmas gift would impress them, or what to say in a card. On-line, it was so much easier to find the right message to type. Because many of her chat-room friends worked during the day, Susan would spend her afternoons thinking up e-mail messages for them to read when they got home.

> *Natalie--I hope your grouchy boss didn't hassle you too much today. Remember that I'm on your side. If you can't stand your job anymore, just quit it and we'll start a business together! Love, Susan.*

> *Leslie--Can't wait to hear about the new bedroom set you picked out. I've already seen from your on-line graphics of your living room that you have a natural eye for decorating. You truly are a woman of many talents! Love, Susan.*

After chatting during much of the night and early morning hours, Susan usually slept until noon and hardly ever left the house to meet with her real-life friends. When she did, she felt distracted with thoughts of meeting up with Natalie, Leslie, and the others when she got back to her keyboard. Her obsession also kept her away from the help wanted ads, a fact that didn't sit well with Richard. She hid the full brunt of her on-line habit from him by saving her longer sessions for those nights he worked late.

Then, unexpectedly, Natalie left Susan this e-mail note: "I'm sorry, but our friendship just isn't right for me anymore, Susan. You're a sweet person and I wish you well, but it's time to move on. This will be the last e-mail I send you."

Susan was devastated. What had she done wrong to push Natalie away? What could she have said to make her angry? Natalie obviously didn't really mean it when she called me a sweet person, Susan thought to herself. She must really hate me. I thought we were best friends, that she was someone I could always count on.

Obsessed with such inner questions and doubts, Susan cried for hours at a time over several days. Then she got up and dug out every printout she had kept from their on-line conversations. She was determined to uncover the clues that would explain where she had failed. She also reread Natalie's final message dozens of times each day, trying to read between the lines to decipher the real message that Natalie was too kind to share.

While this was happening Susan also became more worried about her worsening financial problems from her prolonged unemployment. But if no one really liked her, how could she succeed in the business world, anyway? Her cigarette habit resumed in full force, she reached for the antacid bottle regularly, and she increased her dose of antianxiety medication.

In this desperate state, Susan saw my Internet addiction survey on-line. "Oh boy," she said to herself, "am I the perfect candidate or what? My life is a mess over this." She completed the survey, explaining all the details of the crisis over Natalie. At the end of the survey she added her own message: "Is it normal to feel this way about someone you never met? Am I crazy?"

I assured Susan that her reaction was understandable as a symptom of her Internet addiction and gave her some specific ideas to stop her downslide. I taught her time-management techniques and how to recognize her triggers for addictive behavior. For Susan, this was turning to the computer when she felt tense and insecure; on-line she felt calm and accepted. But to get her past her critical choice points, Susan needed more than positive messages to tell herself. She needed something tangible to keep with her.

## Carry Positive Reminder Cards

I gave Susan these instructions:

- Make a list of the five major problems caused by your addiction to the Internet.
- Make a separate list of the five major benefits of cutting down your Internet use.
- Transfer the two lists onto a 3-by-5-inch index card and keep it in your pocket, purse, or wallet.
- When you hit a choice point where you would be tempted to use the Internet instead of doing something more productive or healthy, take out your index card as a reminder of what you want to avoid and what you want to do for yourself.

Here is Susan's list of Internet problems:

- No job-hunting.
- Lost sleep.
- Ignoring real-life friends.
- Not facing causes of anxiety.
- Secrecy with husband.

This is Susan's list of major benefits of reduced on-line time:

- Pursue job leads.
- Better rested.
- Time to make new real-life friends.
- Find new ways to relieve stress.
- Improve relationship with husband.

The reminders helped. Within two weeks, Susan cut her on-line time in half. But she still struggled to actively pursue some of the benefits on her list. If she didn't see those benefits manifesting in her everyday life, she risked relapsing into excessive usage again. So for Susan, as with many on-lineaholics, it's helpful to map out simple but tangible steps to follow to deal with the problems that sent them rushing toward the Internet in the first place.

### RECOVERY STRATEGY 7:

*Take Concrete Steps to Address Problems*

Susan needs a job. Being out of work was making her more and more tense about money, and less confident of her ability to succeed in her field. Her unemployment also caused a greater strain in her marriage. If I were Susan's therapist, I would help her decide on one concrete step she would take every day to find work. That might mean making one phone call about a job opening, revamping her resume, or writing an old contact in the field to ask about other leads. After she took that concrete step, she could allow herself to use the Internet for a specific time period, perhaps an hour, as a reward.

The concrete job-looking steps need not be limited to studying the job ads, meeting with a career counselor, or pursuing informational interviews at target companies. Susan also might consider using this time at home to explore the possibility of an entirely new career direction. She had achieved some degree of success as a financial analyst, but the pressured environment fed her anxious nature. She was always on edge in the office and agonized over important presentations. On the Internet, Susan especially enjoyed helping people and felt more at ease in that role. Perhaps it was time for her to look into graduate school to become a social worker.

To handle her stress, Susan had turned to substance after substance. I would urge her to set a concrete goal each day of a new and healthier stress reduction technique to research and try. She might begin by playing her favorite soothing music at moments of major stress. She then might try relaxation tapes set to backgrounds of nature sounds, such as bubbling rivers or birds singing. Susan also might check into local groups or classes that teach simple meditation practices. And once she found a tool that clicked for her, Susan could turn to that technique after that one hour she allowed herself on-line as a way to ease back into her real world.

## Computer Crash Frazzles Busy Executive

Max has long felt driven to achieve and succeed. He earned a Ph.D in political science and an MBA. Now he's a busy Chicago executive in mergers and acquisitions. His driving nature has taken its toll: a history of ulcers and migraines, a dependence on sleeping pills, a heart attack five years ago. After plunging into deep guilt and remorse over his recent divorce and impending custody battle for his two children, he was prescribed an antianxiety medication. He travels frequently in his work and lacks the time and patience to form solid friendships and fulfilling hobbies.

This combination of life circumstances made Max a prime candidate for Internet addiction. When he learned the basics of the Internet as a means to track stock market reports and the latest merger news and rumors, he quickly veered down the road of an on-lineaholic. Using the Net for his job was not the problem, of course. But Max also was lured into newsgroups. Within a few weeks, he had signed on to listings for depression, medication, custody fights—the major issues of his personal life. Burying himself in his office more often, Max soon was exchanging e-mail messages with members of more than 30 different groups. Like Wendy and Susan, Max found that talking to others who shared his problems had a calming, numbing effect on him.

"I got completely absorbed in these groups, and when I was there my pain and guilt went away," Max explains. "If one of my groups folded or got boring, I'd immediately find a new one to replace it. It was like having an insatiable thirst and never having enough water."

One day he mentioned his new habit as a joking aside to his psychiatrist, and the psychiatrist told Max about a friend who had left his wife because of her excessive Internet usage. To find out more about this phenomenon, Max quickly went back on-line and joined addiction newsgroups. He began to recognize signs of his addictive pattern. He was spending longer and longer periods on-line, withdrawing socially even more than previously, and now his work was beginning to suffer because of all the office hours on the Internet. During a typically long on-line session, the computer system in Max's office crashed and stayed down for hours.

"I went totally crazy over this," he remembers. "I was pacing all over the building, bugging the systems people to get it fixed, feeling edgy and irritable—just like an alcoholic in withdrawal. I doubled my anxiety medication."

Some time after this incident Max read an article about my study in *The Chicago Tribune* and contacted me to share his experiences. He portrayed himself as an addict already on the road to recovery. He realized he was just using the newsgroups to vent his frustrations over his problems, he told me, so he wasn't solving them. He understood that the Internet had become a major distraction to him. So he had already made decisions to curb his excess use, he claimed. He had reduced the number of newsgroups he belonged to, and he made a pivotal decision—that home computer he had been shopping for so he could use the Internet at home as well as at work was now scrapped. He would only use the Net in his office.

I listened to Max's story and wished him well. Later, I wondered if he still might be operating out of denial of the full scope of his addiction. Driven as always, he appeared in a hurry to pronounce himself recovered. But I wasn't sure he had made the other adjustments that will strengthen his attempts to moderate his use and steer clear of addictive tendencies.

I wasn't convinced that Max really believed he was facing a significant problem. He may have looked upon his dependence as a minor obstacle he could rise above with his basic ability to achieve and succeed—just another business deal to wrap up quickly. But for Max, as with any on-lineaholic, to regain control over the Internet and your life requires a full admission that Internet addiction can be as serious as any other addiction.

## RECOVERY STRATEGY 8:
### Listen to the Voices of Denial

Many on-lineaholics resist the need to seek assistance because of their basic denial of the problem. To uncover your own denial, or help a loved one see it, read these typical statements of denial which have been broken into basic categories so you can understand the specific form of denial. Check each statement that sounds familiar, something you or the Internet addict in your life has said at least once.

## STONEWALLING

___ I don't have a problem with using the Internet.

___ I am not hooked on the Net—I can quit any time I want.

___ Leave me alone; what I do on the computer is my business.

___ I'm not hurting anyone using the Internet.

## MINIMIZING

___ Sure I use the Internet a lot, but it's not a big deal.

___ Hey, it's just a machine.

___ It's not really extramarital sex, it's just words on the computer.

___ My grades are poor because classes are boring, not because I use the Internet.

___ It was just one large credit-card bill (for on-line services). I've spent money on sillier things.

___ It will be all right if I just cool it on the chat rooms for a while.

___ At least using the Internet is not as bad as _____.

## BLAMING

___ It's not the Internet, it's the stress in my life.

___ My wife (or husband) drives me to spend all my time on-line.

___ It's not my fault, it was _____ that got me hooked on this.

___ I need to use the Internet to deal with _____.

## EXCUSING

___ It's been a long day, and the Internet helps me relax.

*continued on page 86*

*continued from page 85*

\_\_\_\_ I must be okay using the Net all night—I still do well in school (or work).

\_\_\_\_ Dad uses the Internet, why can't I?

\_\_\_\_ My life is so hectic, I need this computer world for fun.

## RATIONALIZING

\_\_\_\_ I'll quit the Internet tomorrow.

\_\_\_\_ I deserve a reward for all I've done today; I'll go on-line for a few hours.

\_\_\_\_ Bill Gates uses the Internet, so why shouldn't I?

\_\_\_\_ Getting hooked on the Net is not as bad as drinking or doing drugs.

\_\_\_\_ The on-line fees have gone down, so I can use it more often.

\_\_\_\_ I can learn more in one hour scanning information on the Internet than I ever could in class tomorrow or from reading a book.

\_\_\_\_ The Internet is the only place I meet any real friends.

\_\_\_\_ I can spend time with _____ (spouse or family member) any time, but I only get to talk to my on-line friends at certain hours.

\_\_\_\_ I can't understand why my husband (or wife) complains when I'm on the Net—we don't do much together anyway.

\_\_\_\_ Doing chores is just not as important as staying on-line longer.

\_\_\_\_ So I miss a few hours sleep from the Net; that's just wasted time anyway.

## ATTACKING

\_\_\_\_ You've got a lot of nerve talking about my Internet use.

*continued on page 87*

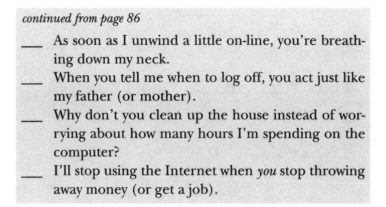

*continued from page 86*

\_\_\_\_ As soon as I unwind a little on-line, you're breathing down my neck.

\_\_\_\_ When you tell me when to log off, you act just like my father (or mother).

\_\_\_\_ Why don't you clean up the house instead of worrying about how many hours I'm spending on the computer?

\_\_\_\_ I'll stop using the Internet when *you* stop throwing away money (or get a job).

If you checked off at least two or three of these typical statements and realize you've been repeating them often, you've been in denial about your Internet addiction. Next time you find yourself making the same comment to deflect attention away from your addictive behavior, you'll be more likely to recognize it as denial. And if you've seen your actions and life circumstances portrayed in the case studies in this chapter, you will be better equipped to see the full impact of your problem and do something about it. Your denial already may be melting.

# FOUR

# The Faceless Community

*Computer networks isolate us from one another, rather than bringing us together*—CLIFFORD STOLL, AUTHOR *OF* SILICON SNAKE OIL

It's Christmas Day at the home of Brett and Nancy and their two children in Omaha, Nebraska. Nancy's cooking Christmas dinner, and daughter Alicia, age seven, and son David, age four, are playing with their new toys amid mounds of crinkled wrapping paper. Brett is alone in the den surveying this message on his computer terminal:

> *You are standing in the northern prayer chamber of the Citadel of Fharlanghn, one of the many worship chambers where the citizens of Corinth can come to worship their mighty deity and praise him for his goodness. There is a 14-foot statue of the Dwellers on the Far Horizon. Many loyal citizens bow down and pay homage to this replica of Fharlanghn.*
>
> *Huge steps lead down through the grand Citadel gate, descending the hill upon which the Citadel is built and ending at the entrance hall below. Prayer chambers of the Citadel lie to the north, east, and west. The year is 539. It is the first day of the month of the shadows. You are Tipper, a 96-year-old man. Other characters are Makr, Deathstalker, Effie, Cheech, Luke, Javiar, Akasha, Sunsword, and Xixor. The gods present are Rosco, Zeus, and Ileah.*

Brett has just entered the Statute Chamber of Meat MUD, a popular Internet interactive game. In this chamber and several others like it, Brett will spend the next several hours hunting gold and other treasures, killing creatures, declaring his undying love to fair maidens, and hobnobbing with the likes of Effie, Sunsword, Xixor, and many other characters who will join the game on this busy Internet day. In real life, these characters are doctors and poets, lawyers and mechanics, college professors and college students. While they're pretending to be heroic characters in the year 539, their real families are in the next room singing and laughing with holiday merriment.

## VICARIOUS PARADISE

"I found more than a hundred people from all over the world logged on to the game on Christmas," Brett relates. "Everyone I ran into during the game was so happy that they could find their friends to be with on Christmas. It was an especially lively game that day. No one seemed in a hurry to leave."

For those addicted to the Internet, an imaginary world like Fharlanghn has become a more attractive holiday hangout than their own living rooms. The friends they know only through words on a computer screen merit as much or more of their time and attention as their own families and actual friends they know by real name, face, personality, and life history. The community they've cultivated through fantasyland interactive games, daily newsgroup messages, or late-night social chat rooms appear stronger, safer, more fun, and more dependable to these on-lineaholics than any work, social, church, or neighborhood community.

Through Internet groups, they've learned that you can do things like climb in a virtual hot tub with hundreds of other users from several countries, pouring champagne into the already bubbling water and massaging the toes of the sexy woman or man across from you. The Webchat Broadcast System, which boasts of móre than a million members worldwide, recently invited everyone on-line to attend the grand opening of the WBS Bar & Grill on St. Patrick's Day. "Drinks and green chat will flow! Bring your derby!" the message read. And these virtual partygoers would be guaranteed to wake up the next day hangover-free.

So when a holiday such as Christmas beckons, Internet addicts just naturally go where the action is, choosing to share the time with those they feel closest to—fellow on-lineaholics. Or when they've just awakened on a typical day, they rush to their e-mail first thing, hoping to find a special good-morning greeting from a chat-room friend. If they find it, they warm to that message more passionately than a good-morning kiss from their lover or the smell of fresh coffee brewing in the kitchen. When they get home from work, they head straight for the computer and eagerly read the typed reports of what happened that day in the lives of their on-line friends, and they offer those faraway people more patience and undivided attention than they extend to those living under their own roof, whose routine stories of work or school now seem stale and predictable. And in their precious leisure time, Internet addicts regularly ignore friends and family to visit their on-line pals.

It's not just a matter of time and attention. Internet addicts often choose their on-line friends to share their darkest secrets, their deepest desires, or just those simple moments that make life vivid and meaningful. They turn to one another as confidants, sounding boards, or even lifelines of support.

But while Internet addicts may benefit from a degree of comfort and support from the words on their terminals, eventually they discover that you can't pull a lifeline through a computer screen. As we will see, those who rely on a faceless community eventually run smack up against the Internet world's very definite limitations.

## What She Could Only Say On-line

Sandy met Carol only weeks ago in an Internet chat room, but they already consider each other intimate friends. Both stay-at-home young mothers, they spend hours capturing the joys and frustrations of child raising in snippets of e-mail. When Carol's baby daughter, Jessica, recently took her very first step, Sandy heard the news first.

"I'm so excited and so proud of her!" Carol typed. "Leon [her husband] is at work. I tried to call him, but he was unavailable. And anyway, I don't think it means as much to him. I'm so glad you're there to share this with, Sandy. This is one of those moments that make it all worth it, you know?"

"I know just what you mean," Sandy answered back. "This is a big moment. I remember when Amanda took her first step. She looked at me for half a second like she couldn't believe she had done it, and I just melted. Then we both laughed together. It does kind of make up for all those times when you just want to scream."

Sandy also was one of the first to learn that Carol was pregnant again. Both also used their on-line friendship to reveal their nagging doubts about their marriages. Sometimes they were able to communicate these thoughts and feelings while on their computers simultaneously. But even when their schedules conflicted, they kept up their e-mail dialogue. Here's a message Carol left as she headed out the door with Jessica to run errands:

"Hiya, Sandy. You know, Leon isn't very happy about the new baby coming. He really didn't want another child, but I trust that he will accept it soon. My day today is going grocery shopping, trying to figure out a nice meal for this evening. It's our six-year wedding anniversary! I can't believe it has been so long. Anyway, I'll be checking the old e-mail when I get back, looking for your reply."

Sandy found Carol's message when she logged on minutes after concluding a visit with her mother. She quickly zipped off a reply:

"I am sure that Leon will feel better about the baby once the little one is born. I remember how Jeff [Sandy's husband] went through periods like that while I was expecting Eddie when Amanda was three. At least Leon is home often for you. Jeff doesn't get home most days because of his sales job. It gets lonely at night, plus I feel like I do all the handling of the kids alone. I think he shows his love by being a good provider, but sometimes I just wish we could have more romantic evenings together. I've got to run now myself. I'll check in with you later. Hang in there. Love, Sandy."

Carol sent her next message two days later, when both she and Sandy were on-line together:

"Leon got laid off again at his construction job yesterday. That's the second time in the last six months. He's getting more frustrated and sometimes he yells at me in his anger. It's very hard for all of us."

"Mmmmm, you sound stressed," Sandy responded: "What about you and Leon getting a sitter and taking a weekend away, or is that too idealistic? I'd like to talk more but I have to run to pick up Amanda at play practice. They're doing Snow White, you know, and on the ride home I hear all about the dwarfs. Gotta go. Your friend, the Chariot Driver."

On the way to pick up her daughter, Sandy felt guilty at cutting short her e-mail conversation with Carol. She realized that Carol depended on her, and she felt gratified to be able to offer another mother support, encouragement, and understanding. Sandy had been down the road of marriage and motherhood a bit longer than Carol. Maybe she had some wisdom to pass on. It would have been nice to have someone do the same for her a few years ago, she thought.

Several days passed without word from Carol. Usually, each woman allowed the other to respond to the last message sent before e-mailing again, but this time Sandy decided to break the pattern. She was beginning to get worried. She sent Carol a quick message to ask what she was up to these days.

For the next two days, Sandy checked her e-mail about five times every hour. At times, she felt even more worried. Other times she wondered if Carol had simply had enough of their friendship. This was Sandy's first experience playing on-line confidante, and she didn't know the rules or what to expect. Maybe people just get close through this computer talk for a while and then they disappear forever, she thought. She never believed Carol would act that way, but now she wasn't so sure. Finally, a new e-mail flashed in Sandy's mailbox:

"Sandy, I'm so sorry I haven't been able to get back to you for so long. I was in the hospital and I just got home today. I got a broken rib from falling down the stairs. I told my mother, the doctor, and all my friends here that it was an accident. But, oh god Sandy, it was really Leon. He hit me and knocked me down the stairs. Fortunately, the baby is still okay. Sandy, you're the only one I can tell this to!"

Sandy was shocked. She and Jeff had their arguments like most couples, but they never came close to violence.

She knew that Carol and Leon had problems, and Carol had mentioned his yelling. But knocking her down a flight of stairs and breaking her ribs? Hitting his pregnant wife? It was too horrible to imagine. And now that this had happened, Sandy wondered, what could she do about it?

After all, Sandy lived in Oklahoma and Carol lived in Pennsylvania. She couldn't just rush over to Carol's house, give her a hug, make her a cup of coffee, run a few errands for her. She couldn't sit with Carol and talk to her face-to-face, helping her decide what steps to take next. She couldn't volunteer to take care of Jessica while Carol was sorting things out. She couldn't meet Leon to size him up, try to understand how he could have done this, or have the chance to say anything to him herself. She wouldn't even know what police department to contact. And if Carol chose to leave Leon for a while, Sandy couldn't even drive her to a battered women's shelter or to Carol's mother's house. Sandy realized that she and Carol hadn't even swapped addresses or phone numbers. All she could do was type e-mails of caring and support.

And what should she say in those messages? How far should she go in offering advice? If this had happened to one of Sandy's old friends or her sister in Tulsa, she would know how to respond. She would remember that person's life history and remind her how she had handled tough times before. They could sit together, and Sandy could see the other woman's facial expression when she spoke, extend a hand at the right moment. She also would know the local resources available to seek out active and immediate support, or she'd at least be able to look through the phone directory with the other person right there, urging her to courageously face the truth of domestic violence. She wouldn't feel so helpless, as she did now.

"Carol, I'm so sorry this happened to you," Sandy finally typed. "I can imagine how hurt and scared you must feel. This sounds really serious. Do you have someone you can call and talk to about this—maybe a therapist, a minister, or a crisis hot line for women in your area?"

"I can't, that would just make things worse," Carol responded. "Leon was really shocked at what he had done and swore he would never do anything like that again. He's my husband and the father of my children. I can't jeopardize that. Anyway, you don't know what it's like around here. And you don't know Leon."

She's right, Sandy thought. We had shared what seemed like intimate moments and feelings, but what did we *really* know about one another? She sent Carol a few more encouraging e-mails and again urged her to seek help in her immediate environment before things got worse. After deflecting Sandy's suggestions a second time, Carol simply stopped answering. Sandy never heard from her again.

## CONNECTIONS WITHOUT REALLY CONNECTING

Sandy contacted me some time after this episode. She told me that she had cut down her own Internet usage dramatically, but she still felt guilty and confused about how she reacted to Carol's confession.

"Could I have done more?" Sandy asked me. I assured her that she had responded as best she could under the circumstances. Like Wendy, the single mom with the spiraling depression in the previous chapter, Carol needed to find support in her real world. And she held the ultimate responsibility for making that choice. All Sandy could do from afar was to urge Carol to seek that support, to take that first step. Sandy now understood that as rewarding as their on-line friendship at first appeared to be, it had come with built-in limitations.

Why did Carol only reveal the truth of what had happened via the computer to Sandy, someone she didn't really know? We may infer that she suffered from low self-esteem that made it more difficult for her to find the courage and strength to report this incident of domestic violence. Or she may have worried, realistically, that Leon would become even more violent and dangerous if she sought help. While too afraid to reach out to those in her immediate environment, she didn't want to suffer totally in silence; she still yearned to share the truth of her experience with *someone*. Sandy represented a safe outlet because Carol didn't have to deal with the repercussions of having told someone who could do anything about it.

Talking to Sandy via the Internet, however, may have sidetracked Carol from the harder decision to confront her husband or take the concrete steps to protect herself and change the situation. She may have deceived herself into thinking she *was* speaking up, she *was* doing something, she wasn't hiding or being a victim. This may have been her best effort at a plea for help, but Sandy, unfortunately, really couldn't help much.

The story of Carol and Sandy represents a dramatic example of ordinary people who reach out to the Internet to make connections while never really connecting with the other person in a meaningful, real-life way. My survey turned up dozens of similar scenarios. Why would so many people choose the Internet community to invest their most cherished time and seek the kind of caring, support, and trust that they could be cultivating in their families and friends around them?

In the profile of an on-lineaholic in the last chapter, we saw how Internet addicts with prior psychological or emotional problems use the escape of the Net to avoid facing those problems, turning to the computer to feel better about themselves and gain a respite from their troubling life circumstances, much as an alcoholic turns to drinking to numb his pain. But Sandy had no history of major psychological disorders. She was just looking to chat with another at-home mother. Many other survey respondents got pulled toward the Internet community with no major psychological problem driving them there. Let's look more closely at their life situations, their motivations for going on-line, the rewards they appear to find there, and the downside to their dependence on this faceless community.

## A Companion for the Homebound

Most Internet addicts, you'll recall, get hooked within months of first venturing on-line. Many discover this stimulating new world after a sudden illness or injury has left them home alone. That's what opened the door to the Internet for Reggie, 30-year-old construction worker in Ohio.

Ever since high school, Reggie had taken great pride in his strength, physical conditioning, and his ability to do things with his hands. But when he fell off a platform during construction of a downtown office building, all that changed. After suffering major head and leg injuries, he was laid up for the first time in his life and expected to remain disabled for months.

Soon after the accident, Reggie's parents gave him a computer with America Online. Within days of first venturing inside the chat rooms, Reggie met his first on-line companion, a man about his age in England who had just become disabled from a car accident. Even if they exchanged nothing more than the mundane details of how they passed their day, Reggie welcomed the reassurance that at least one other person in the world could understand how difficult it was to barely have the strength left to send an e-mail.

Next Reggie met Donna, a 38-year-old Boston loan officer. About a year ago. Donna was diagnosed with cancer. During months of chemotherapy treatments, she lost more than 20 pounds from her already thin frame, and all her hair had fallen out. Her mother and ex-husband visited once in a while, but otherwise Donna was seen only by the doctors and nurses on her treatment days, which suited her fine. She didn't want her friends and coworkers to see her like this. Still, Donna did miss the company of others, and after getting a modem for her computer to work part-time from home, she found Reggie.

With Donna, Reggie was able to share his self-consciousness about his disability. He got up the courage to tell her how his head had been shaved from his injury and how awkward he looked trying to walk on his injured leg. As a lifelong single whose social life previously revolved around his fellow construction workers, Reggie never had been very good at sharing any feelings with women, let alone something this personal. But Donna totally understood and told him she didn't care what he looked like. Alone at his computer, Reggie told Donna he loved her.

But his new social life didn't stop there. Reggie regularly passed his daytime hours chatting with other shut-ins from all over the world. He enjoyed finding a fellow Midwesterner in Indiana—Marcie—who recently had brought her mother in to live with her full-time due to her struggles with Alzheimer's disease. A 42-year-old bookkeeper with a previously active social life, Marcie discovered that when she turned down her friends' offers to go out, they soon stopped calling. She found her new Internet companions like Reggie much more dependable.

Reggie loved having so many new friends and enjoyed playing the role of chat-room social organizer. "The Net saved me from a life of complete loneliness," he beams. "Now I keep the computer on all day, like some people do with TV."

## THE COMPANION THAT NEVER SLEEPS

Forty-two percent of my respondents indicated that they do not hold regular jobs, either because they are full-time students, homemakers, or homebound. For those who can't or don't get out much, the Internet offers a relatively easy path to social contact. Thousands of people are roaming around on-line, and almost anyone you encounter probably will stop and chat if you ask them. Anyone you meet could become a "friend" within days, and when that friend isn't available for a night or two, you'll probably find another. This realization can lift the spirits of people like Reggie.

But even for those who do get out into the world every day, Internet friendship beckons with the same ease and convenience. Compared with real-life social contact, the faceless community is the companion that never sleeps. It's faster, simpler, and available at any hour that fits your schedule. It's like running off to your neighborhood 7-Eleven for basic necessities, rather than driving down to the major grocery store and stocking up for a week or longer.

Consider Janice, the management consultant from Chapter 2 who watched chat-room text scroll on her screen in a semihypnotic trance without joining in. She relies on the convenience of the Internet for company because she travels frequently and often arrives home well after midnight. Who's she going to visit or call at that hour, anyway? So she changes out of her business suit into her sweats, pours a glass of wine, rests her voice, and lets her fingers do the talking. While watching that mindless chatter scroll down her screen, she laughs more easily at silly jokes about politicians and TV characters, and when she does get involved she says things she never would say in a sales conference. In fact, the Internet has worked so well in providing basic social stimulation, Janice decided to see if it might help fulfill another major need in her life—romance.

"It's hard to meet men at all with all the traveling I do and the hours I keep," Janice explains. "And when I do meet someone I decide to date, I'm tired of spending a bunch of money on dinners with guys who turn out to be idiots. The newspaper personal ads didn't work, either. You write a letter, you meet the guy, and right away you find you don't have enough in common. So I tried meeting guys on-line through the *alt.personals* listings."

With the rapid pace of cybertalk, Janice was able to ask her prospective Net dates lots of critical questions: What do you do for work? What do you like to do in your leisure time? What are your hopes and dreams for the future? What are your most important values, and what are the habits you're not so proud of? What's your attitude toward sex? Are you open to having children? How did you come to start using the Internet to meet people anyway?

Because she recognized that married men could easily pose as single in cyberspace, she asked for every man's address and phone number, which chased away the unavailable. Janice's lifestyle also made her a fit for cyberspace personals. With her regular traveling for work, she could readily arrange to meet men in far-off locales. After much screening and chatting on-line, she stepped from behind her computer mask to check them out.

In Pittsburgh she met Darrell, who had seemed especially smart and seductive on-line. They had a brief and torrid sexual affair, but the sparkling intelligence he displayed on the Internet began to fizzle in the light of actual conversation. In Boston she met Scott, an accountant with a flair for the romantic who wanted children, as she did. They clicked some in person, but on the third date he got drunk. Her father had been an alcoholic, so that was the end of that romance.

Within weeks she flew to Seattle to meet Alan, the man who most appeared to share her dreams and visions of the future. He was sweet and sensitive, and he even shared her love of murder mysteries. But when they met, Janice found "no sparks." She didn't feel at all attracted to Alan physically, and after half an hour they didn't even have much to talk about anymore. At that moment, Janice realized that the bond she believed they were building through their on-line exchanges simply was not real. It was an illusion.

## CREATING THE IDEAL PERSON

When you see people only through their words on your computer screen, you are free to conjure up your own image of who and what they really are. If he describes himself as good-looking, you imagine Tom Selleck. If he appears honest and says sweet things on-line, you envision Tom Hanks. The sound of his voice, the gaze of his eyes, the way he might touch your hand—you supply those details in your own mind. You give him automatic passing grades at all those initial checkpoints you normally would cross in person. For example, does his smile reflect sincerity or insincerity? When you talk, does he appear to really listen or is his attention easily diverted to someone or something behind you? You can't see this on-line. And because using the Internet often makes you feel calm or even euphoric, you're naturally going to create the ideal person.

But just as real-life friends or potential mates rarely meet our ideal expectations, so too do Internet contacts fade from perfection when exposed to reality. Suddenly face-to-face with our ideal, we're often struck like Janice by the spell the illusion held over us, and we are powerless to adjust to the human flaws and imperfections that stand before us. Even if we never actually meet this cyber-hero or heroine, we're still filling in the blanks of their identity and relating to the person we've created, rather than the actual person who may be sitting at the other computer. And that creation often does something in our on-line relationship that leaves us cold, angry, or lost.

I experienced this disillusionment myself a few years ago, early in my research. While taking breaks from reading the first responses to my survey, I found myself detouring over to *alt.personals*. I needed to understand how they worked, of course, but as I was also single at the time I was curious to see what sort of men I might encounter there.

I never would have answered a personal ad in the newspaper, where anyone with whom you corresponded would expect to meet right away, but this new form of connection appeared harmless and effortless. I felt more in control. I wouldn't give out my last name, my address, or my phone number, and if I didn't like what I read in an e-mail, I simply wouldn't answer back. No explanation would be needed or expected. One day, this personal ad from a man caught my eye:

> *ISO F ["in search of female"] for friendship, romance, and possibly more. I enjoy long walks, candlelight dinners, and weekend getaways.*

This guy is romantic and does not stress physical appearance, I told myself. Those are important qualities to me. So I responded:

> "Hi, I liked your ad. I have never done this type of thing before. I don't know if you might be interested in chatting with me. If so, e-mail me back."
>
> "Hi, I am so glad you wrote. My name is Jerry and I'm 24 and single. I am a computer programmer and don't have the opportunity to socialize much. I enjoy all sorts of things like reading, sports, and of course romance. I would love to share e-mail with you. Please tell me about yourself."

We started with small talk about our interests, hobbies, and backgrounds. I learned how easy it was to share with someone you didn't see. My messages, Jerry's responses—everything came out unfiltered on the computer. No self-conscious glances, no raised eyebrows to register surprise or disapproval. In many ways it was like having a conversation with a part of myself.

Within a week, we were tapping out messages to one another several times a day, beginning each day with a good-morning note and ending with a cozy good-night. Our conflicting schedules and Jerry's limited computer access often led to gaps of a few hours or longer in receiving and responding to an e-mail, which only prompted me to turn to my e-mail more often in eager anticipation. Did he write? Did he respond? A sense of intrigue heightened the experience.

Once, I vented my frustration about a disturbing experience in my postdoctoral work. I quickly apologized for my mood and for dumping my feelings to my on-line companion, but Jerry responded as I would hope my ideal man would:

> "No need to apologize. You can complain about your day to me any time. I just feel bad that we don't live closer. I wish I could give you more comfort."

With that caring note, Jerry had earned my trust. On the computer, his simple words in black and white appeared solid and definitive. In real life, I probably would have been measuring his tone of voice, his facial expression, any nervous movements of his hands, whether he looked me in the eye. But on the Internet, the message appeared to convey everything essential about the messenger. Clearly, I thought, Jerry is a warm and deeply caring person, someone I could depend on. And while I still didn't fully believe in singles services, I said to myself: "Well, you never know until you see."

So after sharing even more deeply about my upbringing in a middle-class family in Buffalo and my personal and professional hopes for the future, I suggested that we arrange a meeting midway between our homes in New York and Ohio. At first, Jerry responded enthusiastically. But before we had settled on concrete plans, an e-mail message I sent to Jerry came back to me: "User Account Unknown."

Oops, must have typed the wrong address, I figured. I tried again, and it bounced back a second time. Distressed, I waited an hour before trying again. Same result. After a few days, common sense finally began to kick in. Jerry's account no longer existed. With a click of his button, "Jerry" had disappeared from my life. And because we still hadn't shared addresses, phone numbers, or even last names, I couldn't track him down to find out what happened, why he had chosen to cut me off.

## THE "WHYS" YOU NEVER LEARN

Had this happened further along in my survey, after I had heard the now-common stories about lying and game playing on the Internet, I would have had some instant suspicions about my e-mail partner. Instead of 24, Jerry might well have been 54—or 84. As one male respondent to my survey later told me of his pattern of cruising the meeting places for cybersex: "I weigh 250 pounds, I'm 49 years old, and I've lost most of my hair. But I tell the women I meet I'm 23, muscular, full head of blond hair and thin. I know they aren't going to have sex with an old fat guy. Everyone makes up things like this."

Rather than being single, Jerry quite possibly was married, which would explain the fear of meeting. In fact, he might not have been a "he" at all. As I now realize, many Internet regulars use these faceless communities to adopt new personas, including those of the opposite gender. Or Jerry even may have been a sophisticated teenaged boy, typing his lines to me with tongue firmly in cheek, delighted to have fooled and embarrassed an adult woman.

But at the time, I just felt the real-life pain, sadness, and confusion over someone I believed to be growing close to me who had swiftly and suddenly left. And I had no means of finding out why. Like Susan in the previous chapter, who couldn't understand why her chat-room friend had ended their relationship without explanation, I even wondered if I had done something wrong, if I had pushed for a real meeting too soon. I reviewed our past e-mail correspondence looking for clues. Of course I didn't find any, and when I soon got over my loss, I was amazed at how quickly I had trusted and poured my heart out to a stranger, how connected I felt to someone I couldn't see, hear, or touch.

Also, I was struck by how different this ending was from any I had encountered in other friendships. I couldn't pick up the phone and call Jerry to talk out what had happened and express my feelings of hurt and disappointment. I couldn't write him a letter to ask him to explain his actions. I had no gifts to return to him as a symbol of closure. I realized that in the faceless community, commitment can be severed with a click of the button.

## SAFETY BEHIND THE SCREEN

In her book *Life on the Screen: Identity in the Age of the Internet,* Sherry Turkle observes that "computers offer the illusion of companionship without the demands of friendship." Whether looking for romance, cruising for cybersex, or simply finding someone to chat with on a lonely evening, Internet users often welcome the freedom from such demands. They prefer not being accountable for their actions. They enjoy bypassing the real effort it may take in their real lives to form a connection and keep it going for a significant time. They thrive in the pinball-like environment of bouncing from one encounter to the next, without having to reveal themselves fully in the beginning or stopping to say good-bye when they leave. In fact, they don't even have to be seen walking away. They just disappear. Or, if they decide to extend basic chatroom courtesy, they can type a quick log-off message, as "Flamingo" did in the following chat room excerpt:

> LOTUS: *I just had an interview for a job at New Mexico State last week.*
>
> BINKS: *I wish for your dream to come true. I live in Denver now and I believe the Southwest, particularly New Mexico, is magic. What department?*
>
> LOTUS: *The library, I'm a librarian.*
>
> ARRA: *Someday I'll be in New Mexico, too.*
>
> FLAMINGO: *I always wanted to be a librarian but I never lived near a library science school.*
>
> ARRA: *But for now I'll go where I need to go. I have my application in at the Peace Corps, and I'm just waiting to see where they send me.*
>
> LOTUS: *I offer library assistance to Arra whenever needed.*
>
> FLAMINGO: *Well kids, my dog is about to explode, think I'd better walk her and then get to sleep.*

Flamingo may or may not have a dog—no one in her chat room would ever know. She really may have been heading toward bed, or she may have found this conversation boring and skipped to a more stimulating chat room. Or she may have felt jealous of Lotus for landing a job and moving to an exciting new home when she felt stuck in her accounting position for a utility company. The anonymity of the chat room protected her from revealing any of that.

On the flip side of shielding the truth, if you get angry or simply disagree vehemently with something someone said on-line, you can write the source the nastiest response: "You are a blankety-blank idiot. Even my dog has more sense than you!" Internet users call this *flaming*, and in some circles of the faceless community it's regarded as an art form. Of course, the flame-thrower quickly exits the scene, never to return again, at least not under the same handle.

Sometimes the easy intimacy of the Internet makes a user feel safe enough to reveal a strong but controversial opinion. But when you can't see the receiver of your opinion, the truth can get you into trouble, as Carl discovered. An advertising executive in New York, Carl found that he could tell his chat-room friend Doreen in Virginia almost anything about politics, money, and people, and she'd listen nonjudgmentally and offer her own opinion. Until, that is, he confided in her his belief that "those black people living in the inner city on welfare is the largest societal problem we have today."

"Uh, Carl," Doreen responded, "I'm one of those people."

"What? You didn't sound black," Carl wrote. "I apologize for any discriminatory comments. I value our friendship. Please forgive me."

# SHY BY DAY, VIXEN BY NIGHT

It's almost midnight and the lobby of People Connection is bursting with people, excitement, and anticipation. Leah has just clicked on and already is engaging in a little harmless flirting. Then she sends a bolder message: "Any guys out there looking for a foxy babe tonight?" Instantly, her screen fills with invitations from eager men from all over the world who urge this "foxy babe" to come to a Private Room for a more intimate "conversation." The erotic dialogue that ensues resembles what's found on 900 phone sex lines, except that no one is paying for this service and both parties enter the exchange as equals. Usually, men dominate the large group in search of cybersex. But as Leah demonstrates every night, those who cruise the hot spots are not all men.

A 32-year-old single librarian from upstate New York, Leah is shy and overweight. In real life, she feels intimidated by men and hasn't had much success attracting them. "My sister Judy got the looks and the personality in the family, while I got the brains," she laments. Now, when Leah enters People Connection seeking quick sexual encounters, she finds herself desired by dozens of men. She's amazed at how brazen she's become, hopping among several "partners" in one night and indulging in sexual acts she had never previously even imagined.

Leah even gets a chance to exercise her natural intellectual prowess. After a sexual encounter, she often asks the guy who he is and what he does. "I was surprised at how many were willing to stay and talk, and impressed by the professional jobs they held and how intelligent they were," she explains. "We had a lot of good talks. It was a lot better than lying in bed afterward having a cigarette."

For Leah, the best part was the morning after. She had no fears of pregnancy or sexually transmitted diseases. She hadn't spent any money beyond her basic on-line fees. She wasn't concerned about one of the men knocking on her door someday or sending unwanted love letters or flowers, because she never shared her phone number or any specifics about where she lived. Her reputation in her real-life community remained intact. No one knew where she had gone or what she had done, or the language she had used the night before. She was still the same shy, quiet, responsible librarian. And after work she could go home and play the vixen again, engaging in dominance and submission under handles like "Super Vixen" or "Madam X."

"I never knew I had this side in me," confesses Leah, echoing many comments from Internet users who engage in the more deviant sexual or violent behavior online. They might never even think of doing what they do on-line in real life, but the safety of the screen allows them to unleash their unconscious desires and act on taboo or forbidden feelings. With titles such as "Virtual Pleasure" or "Fetish Fair," meeting rooms invite users to visit the darkest nooks and crannies of their minds and dive into primal or animalistic adventures.

On-line, you can express whatever impulses you believe you must repress in your everyday life and get the message back that it's perfectly okay in the free-for-all Internet environment. If you've ever consciously or unconsciously imagined hitting your demanding boss, you can go into a MUD and blow up an enemy instead. If you've had images of tearing the clothes off the attractive man or woman next door, you can create a reasonable facsimile for a cybersex encounter. If you wanted to experience what it's like to be bisexual, you go on-line and just do it. And as you engage in fantasy after fantasy, you don't want to let go. Once we bring our unconscious drives to the front, we don't much want to shove them onto the back burner again.

## WHEN THEY'RE CONTINENTS AWAY

When you're engaging in deviant sexual behavior or otherwise acting out of character on-line, you gain an added degree of security if your cybersex partner or intimate friend happens to live a continent away. After brief trysts with men in Germany, Sweden, and England, Leah felt thankful to learn firsthand that the Net truly is a worldwide community.

For the shy, the extra distance provides a reassuring buffer against the prospect of being asked to actually meet in person. For the cautious, loosening personal boundaries becomes even less threatening when you're sitting in your bedroom in Maryland and the other person is in an office in Sweden. You just can't imagine bumping into them at the grocery store. And international cybertalk, whether intellectual or erotic, offers an extra element of mystery and intrigue.

I discovered that the Internet community has a particularly active pipeline between the United States and England. Phil, for example, grew fond of his British friend, Tippy. A salesperson in a men's department store in Wisconsin, Phil had a poor track record with women: married at 21, divorced at 24, a string of rejections in the last six years. But he had better luck with Tippy, a clerk in a London bookstore. Usually nervous around women in person, Phil relaxed while talking to her about books, theater, men's and women's clothes, the weather, and the differences between their cultures. Tippy had been to New York once and found the people rude, but Phil set out to prove how Midwesterners were more friendly and sincere. He often got up at 5 A.M. to exchange e-mail with her during her morning break at the bookstore.

"She was smart and sensitive—my dream woman," Phil concludes. "She was married, but I still couldn't get her out of mind."

Phil didn't admit it, but Tippy's marital status and safe distance probably made her a more attractive friend. They weren't planning to meet. She wouldn't reject him. She was indeed the "dream woman"—he could hold tight to the dream without fear of having it dashed in the light of day.

Mary Lou, the boutique owner and mother of four we visited in our initial tour of Internet addicts in Chapter 1, also went romancing the Net overseas with Brian. She lives in North Carolina, he lives on the outskirts of London and commutes there for his job as an engineer. She's married, he's married. But both experienced a yearning to reach out to other people, and each quickly got hooked on the Internet.

They found each other in a chat room designed for poetry lovers. They exchanged some of their favorites and why they liked them. That opened the door to conversations about their personal lives, and each decided that there was no need to hold anything back. They were, after all, separated by a vast ocean. So feelings of affection soon sprung forth, and they naturally spilled into poetry.

Although their poetic rumblings turned ever more romantic, Brian and Mary Lou made no overtures toward crossing the divide. Neither of their spouses cares much for poetry, art, or music, so Brian and Mary Lou have discovered an outlet for what they had been missing. That's enough for them—so far. In the next chapter, I'll explore what happens when romancing the Net extends into an actual rendezvous, affair, or even the attempt to form a new life together that leads to real-life separation and divorce among couples.

But even as she remained safely behind the wall of Internet safety, Mary Lou admitted that she was neglecting her husband, children, and her work because of her "harmless" obsession with Brian. Through the lens of addiction, we can see that her life had gone out of control. Which brings us back to the question of why. Why, in this case, wouldn't Mary Lou just start a poetry group in her own community?

## Escape, the Drug of the Internet

Sooner or later, the explanation points to the desire to escape. No matter who they are, where they live, or how solid their lives may appear economically or psychologically, Internet users who turn to the faceless community for company, happiness, or relief usually are trying to avoid something or someone they don't want to confront. Mary Lou felt lonely in her marriage, but rather than face her real pain and confront her husband with her deepest needs, she skipped across the ocean for an intimacy substitute. Leah was trying to sidestep the need for sexual touch and real sharing with men by playing on-screen vixen.

Once this clear pattern of escape emerged in my survey, I asked respondents themselves to identify what they may have been avoiding when they leaped from on-line novice to 40-hour zealot. Most could pinpoint something in their lives that they knew they didn't want to face head-on. In compiling their responses, I arrived at this Top 10 list of avoidances:

1. Loneliness.
2. Marital discontent.
3. Work-related stress.
4. Boredom.
5. Depression.
6. Financial problems.

7. Insecurity about physical appearance.
8. Anxiety.
9. Struggles with recovery from other addictions.
10. Limited social life.

In considering the examples of this chapter, we easily can see why loneliness ranked first. Reggie and his chat-room pals were seeking an escape from their lonely, homebound routines. The loneliness of spending all day taking care of young children first propelled Sandy and Carol toward their on-line friendship that quickly took an unexpected and confusing turn. For all her success in her plane-hopping business world, Janice hungered to break her patterns of isolation at home. And I certainly was going through a period of loneliness that con-tributed to my willingness to reach out to Jerry.

Many Internet addicts simply don't realize how lonely they really are until they experience the surpris-ing joy of meeting their first friend in the on-line community. In our technological age, many of us live as hermits, either literally or symbolically. For the home-bound, the closest thing to real human contact may be listening to the answering machine message of a friend or relative who's busy at work. If we need to buy clothes or household furnishings, we can simply thumb through a catalog and place a quick phone order with an operator in some far-off state. If we need to check our credit-card balance, we just dial an 800 number and wade through a set of voice mail instructions for an au-tomated reporting of our payment information and available line of credit.

We live in rapidly shifting neighborhoods in which we may never know the names of the people next door. At work, we're separated from one another by cubicle walls that siphon off noise while shielding us from our coworkers. Much of our interaction with superiors now unfolds through, yes, the computer. After work, we run our errands, seldom engaging in any real interaction with store clerks or street vendors. When we get home, we're reminded that our families have become estranged by divorce, long work hours, Walkmans, and the ever-present TV. Many families hardly ever eat together, let alone stop to spend conscious time talking to one another. Having people around by no means guarantees freedom from intense loneliness.

So when the faceless community beckons with instant companions and the appearance of intimacy, we embrace it not only with all 10 fingers but with full heart and soul. We feel lighter, more peaceful, more welcomed, more wanted, and better understood. We've got friends. People know us. We're part of the in crowd. We can communicate with others whenever we want. We find ourselves saying to ourselves or to others on-line such comments as:

- On the Internet, I am accepted for who I am.
- My on-line companions are my best friends.
- I can open up to people on-line in ways I can't with others.
- My on-line friends find me funny, bright, and charming.
- I am a more exciting and creative person on the computer.

As a member of this community, you discover not only that you don't have to be lonely, but also that you don't have to concern yourself with just what was making you so lonely in the first place. This realization hits quickly. As we've seen throughout this chapter, the path that leads to obsessive involvement with the Internet community usually leads directly to the center of chat rooms and interactive games. Once you get there, you rapidly immerse yourself in this community despite its limitations, its pitfalls, and its addictive nature that pulls you away from your actual life and the people and predicaments you should be facing. You're now escaping them.


## THE THREE PHASES OF ESCAPE

In studying this dynamic among respondents to my survey, I identified three distinct phases that Internet users tend to experience on the road to addiction.


### PHASE I: ENGAGEMENT

You gain access to a computer with a modem, perhaps as a gift from a well-intentioned family member or friend. You learn about the Internet and begin to check it out. Within days or even hours, you find that one on-line application that most attracts you and pulls you toward regular usage. You engage in the MUDs, the chat rooms, or the newsgroups. You develop an identity there.


### PHASE II: SUBSTITUTION

You plunge so deeply into the Internet community that it becomes a substitute for what you didn't have or couldn't find in life. Within a few months or even a few weeks, you have a friend—or many. You've found stimulation, trust, caring, and support. You've got someplace to go, things to do. The people or activities that used to keep you going in life, you now ignore. The Internet world has become an irresistible stand-in.

## PHASE III: ESCAPE

You turn to your substitute community more and more often, for longer and longer periods. You feel calm, peaceful, and happy on-line, where you don't have to worry about your loneliness or other problems. The feelings you experience in the Internet community act as a temporary antidote to any distress, and numb you to the pain. You want and need more. You have developed a dependence. You are escaping from the real world and your life, and the escape can prevent you from changing anything in your real world. You are living somewhere else.

But when you cling to the social presence of the Internet, you're clinging to nothing more than that presence. You're experiencing just one dimension of life, where you see and respond not only to a distorted image of the people you encounter, as we've witnessed, but also a distorted image of life. As Sandy was reminded through her experience with Carol, real friendship takes time, effort, face-to-face contact, touching. Intimacy doesn't come gift wrapped in a few well-chosen lines of an e-mail any more than it does through a flowery message printed inside a greeting card. Emptiness can't be effectively or permanently filled through a night of cybersex, or just knowing that 10 other people remember your on-line handle. Your reliance on the faceless community invariably diverts attention from the real issue of being alone or feeling alone. Breaking your Internet addiction means confronting the issue head-on.

RECOVERY STRATEGY 9:

*Confront Your Loneliness*

We all need the presence of real people and engagement with them to fulfill the richer emotions of life. That's how we grow. But it all can seem so frightening and intimidating, full of the kinds of challenges that we try to avoid on the Internet, where we have time to read every message and calmly and privately think of the right words to say in reply. In real life, even a shrug of the shoulder can convey a deep feeling, real or imagined by the other person. We also initiate responses when we change the tone or inflection of our voice. An insecure person can be especially sensitive to stern words spoken loudly.

And these are just the challenges most often associated with initial social contacts. Actually getting to know someone and building a long-term friendship or intimate relationship carries a whole new set of tough tasks and decisions. How often do you meet? How much do you talk on the phone between times in person? Who calls whom? Do you go to the new club for a drink or to a movie? How do you demonstrate your caring or affection—words, gifts, hugs, opening your photo album? When do you touch and how much?

If you're living with loneliness, you're probably missing out on these simple choices and moments that build true closeness. If you depend on the Internet community for human contact, you're still avoiding those challenges. You grow accustomed to friendships and contacts that happen almost in a blur. On-line relationships take on the form of a fireball; they ignite quickly, but they just as rapidly fizzle and burn out. In real life, most connections start and end much more gradually, with slower warm-up phases and slower cooldowns. So they're much harder. That, ultimately, is what Internet addicts may be escaping—the hard work of being human. To begin to take on that hard work and confront your loneliness, here are a few guidelines.

1. *Transfer positive qualities.* If you've been mainly an introvert and have used the Internet to find yourself and

begin to climb out of your shell, you may have made a positive first step. But instead of limiting your social life to the faceless community, move on to real-life situations. Wouldn't it be nice to have that kind of caring, support, trust, and affection from people you could see and touch? To reach out to them, remember what people responded to in you while you were on-line and popular. Did they find you witty, caring, attractive, and intelligent? Well, you have those qualities and you bring them with you wherever you go, even when the computer is off. Now you have the chance to transfer those feelings into encounters with real-life people.

Visualize yourself acting with the same positive qualities in a typical social situation you might face at work, school, or even at the grocery store. Think of yourself recapturing those same feelings you had when people liked you on-line and you reveled in their company and attention. You can begin to receive them from real people now. Imagine how empowered you will feel if someone really *sees* you and still thinks you're great. And if you could navigate the Internet to find the places that most engaged you, you can weave through social groups to find where you soon will fit in.

2. *Change your situation.* Look at the circumstances of your life and how they may be contributing to your loneliness. Is it time to move out of your isolated rural environment and come closer to a more stimulating city? Will a job change that reduces your travel or overtime open the door to more social opportunities after hours? Joining a new social group or club, even one that only meets for two hours once a month, can provide you with new friends who share your interests and fears. Or maybe you had a support network that you unintentionally aban-

doned when you got so engrossed in the Internet. You can go back again.

Perhaps it's a physical situation that needs a change. If you avoided real-life contact because you are overweight, use your excursion into the anonymous Internet community as a launching point to do something about your health and appearance. Let the feelings of acceptance you found on-line inspire you to eat better foods, adopt a sensible diet, and exercise regularly so you look and feel better. When you wear that same attractive glow in your fitness club that people saw in the chat rooms, you'll be just as desired.

3. *Explore the difficult feelings.* If you turned to the Internet because a sudden accident or illness left you homebound, you've probably got some strong emotions stirring inside you. You may even notice that in addition to burying yourself in the computer for hours, you're also drinking or smoking more in response to the trauma. But like those other drugs, the Internet is a short-term fix. If you're still relying on the same crutches after a month or two, recognize that the Net has not really helped and that you need long-term assistance to cope with your problem or disability.

You may want to seek a job. More and more people with disabilities, even severe ones, are being welcomed into the world of work. The benefit is not only financial. Real social contact may lift your spirits and make you less vulnerable to the lure of the faceless community.

You also may benefit from a support group for people in your same situation, or from doing volunteer work for those trying to overcome comparable hurdles. Psychotherapy may emerge as the best option to uncover and express all those feelings of anger, fear, or embarrassment. If you are seeking psychological help for the first time and you're self-conscious about how to begin to explore some of these issues, bring in this book and mention it to your therapist. It will be a useful starting point.

# FIVE

# Cyberwidows:
# Victims of Terminal Love

*When my husband was home before, he was* home . . .
*now he can be gone for hours, lost in e-mail.*
—*A WASHINGTON, D.C., WRITER, QUOTED*
*IN* THE WALL STREET JOURNAL

The most difficult moments during my study emerged from witnessing the anger, frustration, confusion, and pain of the women and men whose spouses' on-line habits had threatened or destroyed long and apparently stable relationships. Every week, I'd receive more of their e-mail notes, telephone calls, and letters, and I'd be touched by their heartfelt pleas for help. Something new and frightening had crept silently into their lives, and they didn't know what to make of it or do about it. Through simple words on a computer screen, another man or woman had invaded their homes and their lives. Within weeks of breezy Internet chatting, terminal love had struck with the force of a tornado, leaving cyberwidows trying to dig out from under the real-life rubble.

In this chapter, we'll look at the warning signs that tell you a cyberaffair could be about to blow a hole through your marriage. When you learn those signs and watch for them, you'll understand better what's happening to your Internet-addicted spouse and be prepared to take action to head off serious damage. But what if terminal love already has begun to take hold, and while you're feeling its serious effects, your spouse insists that nothing's wrong or simply wants to leave the marriage without talking about it? We'll cover the steps to follow in confronting your avoidant spouse and taking care of yourself and your needs.

First, I'll share a few of those messages I've received from cyberwidows. As a person living with an Internet addict who has turned to the computer for intimacy, you may see or hear yourself in their stories. Or, if you're the on-lineaholic who has strayed from your marriage with late-night hideaways in Romance Connection or a string of cybersex one-nighters, you may hear in another voice the pain you're causing in your marriage. Here's a sampling of real e-mails that I received. Only the names are changed.

*Dear Dr. Young,*

*My name is Dennis. I have been married for eleven years, and my wife, Melinda, and I have three children. We bought a new computer a few months ago, and Melinda got very interested in the chat rooms. Soon the friendly chat turned to cybersex, and from there it escalated into phone sex. Finally, she started driving to meet a couple of these guys hundreds of miles away, taking the children with her! When I found out about this and confronted her, she refused to admit she had a problem. I filed for divorce, but I'm afraid she's going to take the kids and move far away. I'd appreciate any advice you could offer.*

*Dear Dr. Young,*

*My name is Beth and I live in Maine. Today, my husband of 12 years told me he's leaving to go live with a woman in Iceland whom he met on the Internet three months ago. I am shocked! The have never met in person--my husband has never even been out of the country. Now she's finding him a job in Iceland and he's leaving tomorrow. How could this have happened? What do I do?*

*Dear Dr. Young,*

*Reading your Web site about Internet addiction this morning was the answer to my prayers. My husband Bill is addicted to chat centers. Bill is very gregarious. I didn't mind when he just talked to other women on the Net. But the conversations turned sexual, and Bill was fired when he got caught swapping e-mail love notes with his on-line lovers at work. He went to therapy, but quit after four sessions. Bill says he loves me and he's trying to stop, but he continues to sneak around electronically. I am angry, bitter, and suspicious. Although I've been with Bill for over two decades, and want to help him through this, I'm fed up with the deception. Can you help?*

*Dear Dr. Young,*

*My wife spends more than 40 hours a week playing these fantasy role-playing games on the Internet. Her "virtual life" has left our marriage and family in shambles. All she wants to do is play the game. A man she met on-line got her address and is sending her very strange and personal letters. I'm afraid she may leave. Our pastor does not know how to help. Can you suggest anything I can do to bring her back to reality? Our whole family is really hurting . . .*

When I first received these distress calls, I was amazed that men and women actually were leaving their spouses to run away with someone they had never even met. But as the contacts from cyberwidows multiplied and the stories began to take a familiar form, at least I was prepared for what I would hear. More important, I could offer cyberwidows the validation they had been hoping to find.

"You are not alone," I would assure them. "What you're telling me, I've heard before. This is happening to more and more people out there."

I would ask them questions about their spouse's behavior in the period leading up to the discovery of the cyberaffair: Did you notice him doing this? Did you hear her doing that? With few exceptions, they would answer affirmatively. Through their feedback, I gained a clearer understanding of the dynamics of Internet relationships. Now I recognize the common signals that an on-line romance has ignited.

*Learn the Seven Warning Signs of Terminal Love*

If you suspect that your spouse or partner has found love on the Internet, ask yourself whether you've seen the following signs in their behavior:

1. *Change in sleep patterns.* As we've seen, chat rooms and meeting places for cybersex don't heat up until late at night, so on-lineaholics tend to stay up later and later to be part of the action. If your partner suddenly begins coming to bed in the early-morning hours, long after you've turned in, there's a good chance that cyberlove is brewing. Similarly, if he or she sometimes leaps out of bed an hour or two earlier and bolts to the computer, a prework e-mail exchange with a new romantic partner may explain things. Or if the cyberlover lives several time zones away, this may be the only time for live computer interaction.

2. *A demand for privacy.* If someone begins cheating on his or her partner, whether on-line or in real life, he or she will often go to great lengths to hide the truth from

CYBERWIDOWS: VICTIMS OF TERMINAL LOVE    *125*

the partner. With terminal love, this attempt usually leads to the search for greater privacy and secrecy surrounding computer usage. Maybe he's moved the computer from the visible den to a secluded corner of his locked study. Perhaps she's changed her password in fear that her husband knew the old one. Or, where he used to share some of what he was doing on-line and whom he met there, he now cloaks all his activities in secrecy. And when they're on-line, cheating cyberlovers do not want to be disturbed or interrupted—that might lead to getting caught.

3. *Household chores ignored.* When any Internet user increases time on-line, household chores often go undone. That's not automatically a sign of terminal love, but in a marriage those dirty dishes, piles of laundry, and unmowed lawns might indicate that someone else is competing for the suspected person's attention. In an intimate relationship, sharing chores often is regarded as an integral part of a basic commitment. So when a partner begins to invest more time and energy on-line and fails to keep up his or her end of the household bargain, it could signal a lesser commitment to the relationship itself—because another relationship has come between you.

4. *Evidence of lying.* Did the credit-card bills for on-line services suggest your wife was spending three times longer on the Net than she claimed? Did your husband swear he was using the Internet only for research for a work project when you know he finished it a week ago? When you walked in the room as your partner was logging off, did she insist she was "just chatting" on-line, when the flushed look on her face suggests a different activity? Most Internet addicts lie to protect their on-line habit, but those engaging in terminal love have a higher stake in concealing the truth, which often triggers bigger and bolder lies—including telling you they will quit.

5. *Personality changes.* Cyberwidows often tell me how surprised and confused they were to see how much their partner's moods and behaviors changed since the Internet engulfed them. A once warm and sensitive wife becomes cold and withdrawn. A formerly jovial husband turns quiet and serious. If questioned about these changes in connection with their Internet habit, a partner engaging in terminal love responds with heated denials, blaming, and rationalization. The cyberwidow is told he or she is the one with the problem, or it's just no big deal. For a partner once willing to communicate about contentious matters, this could be a smokescreen for a cyberaffair.

6. *Loss of interest in sex.* Some cyberaffairs evolve into phone sex or an actual rendezvous, but cybersex alone often includes mutual masturbation from the confines of each person's computer room. So when your Internet-obsessed partner suddenly shows a lesser interest in sex with you, it may be an indicator that he or she has found another sexual outlet. If sexual relations continue in your relationship at all, your partner may be less enthusiastic, energetic, and responsive to you and your lovemaking. She could be expending her real passions on a cyberpartner, or her guilt from carrying on a cyberaffair may leave her not wanting to be touched by you.

7. *Declining investment in your relationship.* Those engaging in terminal love no longer want to do fun things together or go out with you, even when their busy Internet schedule allows. They shun those familiar rituals like a shared bath, talking over the dishes after dinner, or renting a video on Saturday night. They don't get as excited about taking vacations together and they avoid talk about long-range plans in the family or relationship. They're having their fun with someone else, and their thoughts of the fu-

ture revolve around fantasies of running off with their cyberpartner, not building intimacy with you.

Let's look at a typical example of terminal love and its impact on one long-term marriage. I learned of this story from Sarah, who called me the day after her husband, David, filed for divorce. Despite the presence of every warning sign, David had continued a cyberaffair until it had destroyed their marriage. We'll explore how Sarah initially missed the signals and, when she did begin to catch on, how she felt powerless to stop them. We'll also learn why David felt so strongly driven by his computer fantasy. And after we see what went wrong, I'll offer a recovery strategy that you can follow to avoid such a destructive fate in your relationship.

## ROCKING THE BOAT IN CANADA

After 23 years of marriage, David and Sarah finally had time for themselves. Sons Tom and Christopher had grown up and gone off on their own. Thanks to David's success as an engineer, they enjoyed financial security. Sarah also worked part-time at an art museum. They lived in a good home in Toronto and they owned other property in Canada and a beach house on the outer banks of North Carolina, where they spent three weeks every summer and talked of turning it into their retirement home.

Their marriage had endured its ups and downs, and now Sarah yearned for the kind of closeness and enjoyment she remembered from their early dating days as college students. They recently had purchased a boat, which they would take out every weekend. Life, as far as Sarah could see, appeared full of new possibilities.

Eight months ago, David got a new computer and modem with fancy software programs to help manage their finances. He got excited by the Internet's information-gathering power, and every night after dinner he'd spend a couple of hours surfing for investment tips and stock reports. He'd often invite Sarah into his study to show her what he found. She didn't fully understand all the whys and wherefores, but she shared David's enthusiasm for exploring new ways to invest their money. This even may lead to an earlier retirement, she thought.

But after a few weeks, David rushed upstairs immediately upon arriving home from work to fire up the computer, without stopping to offer Sarah so much as a kiss hello. He'd sit there transfixed until dinner time, and then he told Sarah he wanted to eat in front of the computer so as not to break his concentration. This request disappointed Sarah because after the boys had left home, their dinner hour had begun to take the form of a shared ritual. She loved devoting more energy into fixing what her husband most enjoyed. Now, instead of seeing more of him, she saw less.

"Still, I didn't think much of it at first," explains Sarah. "I even started bringing him dinner on a tray. Maybe he needed all this time to get to know how the computer worked, and, anyway, I assumed he was still doing things to improve our financial situation and help us retire sooner. Or this was a new hobby and he'd soon lose interest."

Sarah already had missed a couple of signs that terminal love had come creeping into their lives, or at the very least that David's Internet use was pushing him toward addiction. David had become more withdrawn. That avoidance of a kiss hello could be a tip-off of a changing personality due to what he was doing on the computer. His desire to eat alone may be interpreted as a statement that he didn't wish to participate in the kind of ritual that enhanced intimacy.

Things soon got much rockier. David always had followed an early-to-bed, early-to-rise pattern, but now he was coming to bed after midnight and sacrificing three or four hours of sleep every night. And when Sarah managed to stay awake until he logged off, he usually told her he was too tired for sex. The few times they did make love, David seemed preoccupied. Sarah felt not only unfulfilled but suspicious.

"I even wondered then if he was having an affair," she admits, "but as far as I know he had always been faithful in our marriage. Plus, he came home from work on time and stayed home every night. It didn't add up."

Because she didn't know anything about chat rooms or cybersex, Sarah also missed these clearer signs that David had fallen into terminal love. His sleeping pattern had changed dramatically, and he didn't want to have sex with her. Sarah did suspect an affair but didn't believe it could be possible because she was thinking in terms of real affairs, the kind with phone calls and secret meetings at hotels.

This is where cyberwidows who contact me expressed utter confusion and bewilderment. They tell me that it seemed like something had gone wrong, or that they wondered if their partner could have been engaged in an affair. One suspicious husband even hired a private detective to follow his wife to find out what she was really up to all day while he was at work. The detective didn't have to go far: The woman never left the front of her computer terminal. With this evidence, the husband figured his wife was simply frittering away her time talking to other bored homemakers, and he concluded of his earlier suspicions: "It must be my imagination."

Still other signs slipped past Sarah. David stopped inviting her into his study to show her how the computer worked and to track some of their investments together, explaining that this new financial work was too complicated for her to understand. He'd fill her in later, he assured her. For now, he expected privacy. Sarah found this disturbing because he never had kept their money matters a secret. And where she once relied on him to keep the lawn neatly mowed and the shrubs trimmed, she now found him neglecting all chores. He wasn't even sprucing up their prized boat, and as he spent more weekend days on-line, that boat never got out of dry dock.

## A BEACH BUM'S ULTIMATE FANTASY

The signs had been building for more than six months now, and one night when David went to bed early with the flu, Sarah finally took action. She marched into his study and logged on. Remembering what he had showed her from their earlier computer sharing, she weaved her way into David's files. She stumbled upon one with the subject line "Obsession." Though Sarah didn't understand all the strange computer coding and shorthand, her instincts told her that this message from someone named "Aqua Velvet" was some kind of love letter.

"I went right into the bedroom, woke him up, and asked him what this was all about," Sarah relates. "He admitted that he did play in these meeting rooms late at night sometimes, but it was all done as a joke. He said he couldn't understand why any woman would write him a serious love letter because he had never done anything provocative in the rooms. But he said he was very sorry that it had upset me, that he wouldn't play in the meeting rooms anymore, and that he'd try to get to bed earlier. Looking back at that moment, I wish I had thrown the PC out the window."

Had she come upon this printout of one of David's private chats with Aqua Velvet, which she only found months later, Sarah might have taken that drastic step:

BEACH BUM (*DAVID'S ON-LINE HANDLE*): *Hi there, love.*
AQUA VELVET: *I thought you forgot about our little date.*
BEACH BUM: *I could never forget about you.*

AQUA VELVET: <s> *(a smile)*

BEACH BUM: *You are always on my mind--so how is my lovely lady today?*

AQUA VELVET: *Well, it's been a long day at work and I have to prepare for an important early-morning meeting. And I'm having the kitchen redone tomorrow, so I'll have to rush home before noon and make sure the contractors know exactly what I want.*

BEACH BUM: *Sounds like a lot to handle.*

AQUA VELVET: *Tell me about it.*

BEACH BUM: *You could use a nice dip in my Jacuzzi looking over the beach in North Carolina.*

AQUA VELVET: *Mmmm, that would be heavenly, especially us sipping wine.*

BEACH BUM: *I would pour your wine, and rub your feet under the bubbles, would that relax you?*

AQUA VELVET: *Oh God, yes!!!! <s>*

BEACH BUM: *<wink>*

BEACH BUM: *Yes, I would rub your feet and move up to your wonderful legs, giving just enough pressure--not too hard, not too soft.*

AQUA VELVET: *Oh, I would love that, you are wonderful to me.*

BEACH BUM: *You deserve nothing but the best.*

AQUA VELVET: *I wish my ex-husband had thought that.*

BEACH BUM: *Yes, I would put you on a pedestal and never take you off it.*

AQUA VELVET: *What does the sunset look like there?*

BEACH BUM: *Well, while we sipped wine, we could stare out at the orange-reddish blaze across the sky, with a sliver of the moon perceptible over the ocean, feeling a light breeze.*

AQUA VELVET: *Oh, that sounds great, I would love to lay around watching the sunset over the ocean.*

BEACH BUM: *Weather here is wonderful compared to the north, let's run away together. <wink>*

AQUA VELVET: *Yes, I would be there in a moment--you are such a dear.*

BEACH BUM: *And I could show you how romantic the beach is.*
AQUA VELVET: *Yes, I want to make love on the beach, feeling the warm sand on our bodies.*
BEACH BUM: *It is just a plane ticket away.*
AQUA VELVET: *Oh, yes, to run away from it all . . .*

Without this clear evidence of a cyberaffair, Sarah wanted to believe that David hadn't crossed the line. She gave him the benefit of the doubt about cutting out the late-night flirting, and for a few days he did start coming to bed at a reasonable hour. But soon it was back to the old routine of late nights and extreme privacy. She confronted him a second time, he again swore he'd change, and she told him she would forgive him and stop bugging him if he would just cut down on the Internet and pay her more attention. But it didn't stop, and when she tried to talk to him about it more directly, he became angry and defensive.

"This was not the patient and reasonable man I had known," she said. "Then when I suggested we get into counseling together, he told me I should go alone because the problems were all my mine, that I was just being jealous and demanding, and I probably just felt more lonely because the boys had moved out."

With his refusal to enter marital counseling, David made the final statement of his unwillingness to invest time and energy in their marriage. He kept up the secrets, lies, and denials for a few more weeks, then he finally told Sarah the truth. Yes, he had met someone over the Internet. Yes, he was in love with her. Yes, he was filing for divorce, and in that same North Carolina beach house he and Sarah had shared so many intimate moments alone together and as a family, David was going to start a new life with Janice, the actual woman behind the on-line handle Aqua Velvet.

## WOMAN OF THE WORLD

To David, Janice was everything Sarah wasn't. She was highly educated, with an undergraduate degree in English from Vassar and an MBA from Cornell. She had a high-powered job as a corporate marketing executive in New York, and she had traveled throughout Europe and the Middle East. Like David, she had made a lot of money and she liked to use it to enjoy herself: good restaurants, fine wine, expensive wardrobe. She was also independent, having ended her first marriage when her husband insisted upon children and she wanted to focus on her fast-moving career. Still only 37, she looked to men for shared adventure.

Sarah, in contrast, preferred quieter times and a slower pace. She'd rather cook than eat out, her tastes in clothes were simple, and she never had traveled beyond a few provinces of Canada and their beach house in North Carolina. She never had entertained major career ambitions, and even with her sons grown up she still identified with her role as mother. In her spare time, she enjoyed making crafts, shopping, and greeting museum visitors. To David, she now seemed boring and predictable.

In her spare time, Janice loved to go rock climbing, skydiving and hang gliding, the sort of activities that Sarah would find terrifying. Janice also appeared more interested in hearing David's dreams, including the ones he gave up when he got married in college. Adding to the allure, she asked David to tell her about his erotic fantasies and she shared her own with him—their cyber-sex got pretty wild. He couldn't imagine talking that way to Sarah.

Clearly, David was creating the ideal person in the manner we discussed in the previous chapter. He still hadn't met Janice, but he was filling in all the blanks to conform to the ideal. Not only was Janice a passionate risk taker, he decided, she also must be kind, caring, supportive, honest, and flexible. How could any spouse compete with such a fantasy image?

In the instant and anonymous intimacy of terminal love, David revealed only an idealized image of himself. He emphasized his success as an engineer and his knowledge of the world of investments. He talked often of his great love for the ocean and boats, and to demonstrate his spirit of adventure he told Janice of his dream of building his own sailboat and sailing around the world. And, of course, he would show Janice through his typed messages that he was sensitive, witty, generous, and dependable. No need to mention his latest penchant for secrecy, lies, and insensitivity toward his wife, not to mention ending, with so little integrity, a 23-year relationship.

Would this new union between Janice and David last beyond their initial meeting at the beach? I heard of many cases of seemingly perfect terminal love among both married and single cyberlovers that instantly failed as real-life relationships. Stripped of their fantasy masks, cyberlovers seldom embrace the other person when they discover how he or she really looks, acts, feels, and talks, and they catch on to the bigger lies easily concealed from the safety of the computer. I never heard from David, but later in this chapter we'll visit with Anne, a woman who left her husband for a cyberlover and broke off the new relationship within weeks.

I can't say that Internet-born unions never work. Through the media, we occasionally hear about single men and women who do find true love on the Net and marry their cybermate in real life. A few even choose to go back to their separate computer stations to type their legal wedding vows on-line. But a more likely Internet romance scenario, especially for married men and women cruising cyberspace for affection, is what Abigail Trafford described in her book *Crazy Time: Surviving Divorce* as a *coup de foudre*, or bolt of lightning romance. Like a teenager, you tumble instantly into love and get swept away with the image of living happily ever after. But the passion fizzles almost immediately, and the experience is understood best as avoidance of the marital discontent you had kept simmering inside.

## SARAH, AN ENABLER OF ADDICTION

Through the lens of a cyberwidow, it's easy to judge David and blame him for the breakup of his marriage with Sarah. But in my experience studying terminal love from all perspectives, I learned that the partner of the Internet wanderer usually plays a role in the breakup. Addiction counselors have alerted us to the role of enablers, partners of alcoholics who inadvertently allow the irresponsible or destructive actions of the addict to continue. Usually well intentioned, the enabler at first glance appears to be acting in a supportive or even nurturing manner. With Sarah, we witnessed her willingness to deliver her husband's dinner to his study on a tray, so he could keep working on the computer. She told me that she felt then like she had years earlier when she used to bring snacks to the boys while they did their homework.

Enablers usually lack the self-esteem to assert their own needs, so they seek respect and validation through a caregiving role, and by assuming more responsibility in the relationship. Sarah not only sacrificed those intimate dinners to let David enjoy his new hobby, she also began to take care of all the chores he neglected. She even invented excuses for him when other couples called to invite them on boating outings or other weekend activities. "He's just real busy on a new project," she would say.

Enablers see themselves as victims, powerless to change the other person or the behavior causing them pain. For several months, Sarah said nothing to David about his Internet obsession until she stumbled upon evidence of his betrayal. Even then, she was quick to accept his half-hearted denials of his romantic endeavors and willing to believe his vows to curb his habit. When he "fell off the wagon" and returned to his midnight liaisons, Sarah quickly lapsed into an unhealthy cycle: He'd assure her that it wouldn't happen again, she'd forgive and go on until his on-line time escalated again. Only after her own life had veered out of control did she suggest marital counseling, and by then David was polishing up his getaway plans.

From the start, Sarah faced enormous challenges in responding to David's behavior. Unlike enablers of alcoholics, she didn't know she was dealing with an actual addiction. Unlike spouses who catch their husbands or wives in open adultery, she only knew that David was sharing intimate words with another woman on a computer. And as we noted, she didn't know the warning signs of terminal love. But if you are a cyberwidow today or suspect you may be one, you can make more informed choices and act to intervene more swiftly and successfully.

Anyone living with a person whose life has been consumed by an addiction has the opportunity to plan and execute an intervention. With an alcoholic or drug addict, the intervention usually entails a meeting with the person's entire family. A few select close friends and perhaps clergy or a therapist also may attend. Everyone tells the addict of their feelings of anger and pain caused by the addict's behavior, along with specific examples of just what the addict has done to hurt them while drunk or stoned. The intervention participants also declare their love for the addict and their support in helping the addict face the illness. Usually, the intervention ends with the group urging the addict to begin an addiction treatment program immediately.

Intervention with an Internet addict requires a different plan, because abstinence is not necessarily the aim. Although some change clearly is desired by the cyberwidow, it's up to that person to decide what form the change should take. Also, terminal love usually affects only the couple in real-life relationship together. Far from calling a wider meeting of family and friends, the cyberwidow more likely will be going it alone, at least at first. So he or she needs to take great care in the approach to the Internet addict and call upon only the most effective communication tools.

## RECOVERY STRATEGY 11:

### *Follow the Seven Steps of Communication*

If you know or suspect that you are a cyberwidow, you can respond to the seven warning signs of terminal love by taking these seven steps to communicating with your partner.

1. *Set your specific goals.* What do you really want? Do you just need your partner to end the cyberaffair while you still allow an occasional cybersex dalliance, or do you want all communication with the other person terminated as a solid gesture to begin rebuilding your trust? Are you hankering to pull the plug completely on all Internet use, and if so, are you prepared for your partner's likely withdrawal to hit? If you adopt a more modest goal of time moderation, how many hours per week would you aim for—25 or 5? Do you want him or her to limit Internet usage to weeknights, with weekends free to spend together, or are you willing to grant one on-line weekend day with the assurance that you will have one shared

weekend day to go out and have fun or just spend quiet time at home?

Think about what you're really looking for in the relationship, beyond the changes you will request regarding Internet usage and activity. If you've struggled to ask for your needs to be met previously, this Internet-triggered crisis could provide an opening for you to become more clear and assertive about the kind of intimacy you seek. Use the opportunity to do some real soul-searching before you approach your partner.

2. *Find a good time to talk.* The worst time to approach an on-lineaholic is when she or he is at the computer. Interrupting during the height of a cybersex encounter would be especially embarrassing to your partner, and you'd both likely begin your communication with anger and hostility—not the best conditions for a fruitful dialogue. Plan for a wide window of time to share openly and honestly, when the distractions of home and family life are minimized.

Many cyberwidows complain that because their partner is *always* on-line, they can never find a moment to approach him or her. I often suggest approaching the person just before he or she normally would go on-line, with a simple and direct overture like: "Before you log on, I need to talk to you for a few minutes." This is preferable to waiting until 2 A.M. when the offending partner comes to bed; by then you're both tired and you've been seething with resentment for the last several hours. There may be no perfect time, but whenever you approach your partner, you want to be clear, calm, and rested.

3. *Decide what you most want to say.* Just as you need to be specific about the changes you're asking for, you need to be specific regarding just what behavior is upsetting to you, exactly how it affects you, and when you've experi-

enced the pain. Sarah, might have told David how much she values their dinners together and how much she missed them, or about her anger at picking up the slack over the chores, her disappointment about an empty sex life, her sadness over the end of their boating excursions.

Recall actual incidents where your partner let you down—the movie he wouldn't go to with you, the dinners she no longer prepares. Think about how your partner's behavior has affected you in your own moods and behavior. Are you losing sleep because you're upset with what's happening? Do you feel more irritable or angry? Are you worried about where your relationship is going? Again, this is an opportunity to share your deepest troubles and concerns in the relationship.

4. *Use nonblaming "I" statements.* Use nonjudgmental language that won't sound critical or blaming. If you say, "You never pay any attention to me because you're always on that damn computer," your partner will perceive it as an attack and become defensive. Instead, use "I" statements that communicate your experience and your feelings. "I feel neglected when you spend long nights on the computer" or "I feel rejected when you say you don't want to make love to me." If you suspect terminal love but don't have hard evidence, avoid an attack posture that says. "You're screwing around with women all night in those sex rooms and I've had enough of it!" Instead, speak to your real concerns: "I feel hurt that you don't want to talk about our future plans anymore, and I wonder if you've met someone else through the computer."

Stay focused on the present experience. This isn't the occasion to bring up other time-consuming hobbies or obsessions your partner used to indulge in; that only sounds judgmental. Stick with what's happening with the Internet, and avoid trigger words such as *always, never, should,* or *must.* They sound inflexible and invite heated rebuttal. Stick to simple statements of what you know or what you feel.

5. *Listen empathetically.* When your partner does respond, stop and listen fully and respectfully. Try to suspend your point of view momentarily and walk in his or her shoes. Taking this approach does not mean that you lose yourself or agree with your partner's assertions or perspective. Rather, you are demonstrating that you're open to what he or she says and are trying to accept that reality without condemnation.

Your receptivity may allow your partner to open up about why he or she has stumbled into a web of terminal love, and you may be surprised by what you hear. Many Internet addicts explain that they never sought cyberaffairs but found the process happening too fast for them to see and understand. Underneath, they may be feeling guilty and truly wish to stop. Or the cyberflings may have stirred up their own resentments about the pain over what's been missing for them in your relationship. Without suspending your feelings of betrayal or loss of trust, without dropping your need to see your partner make real changes, try to listen to these explanations as openly as possible. Remember that your facial expression and body language also communicate your receptivity or lack of it. Unlike Internet encounters, your communication is multidimensional!

6. *Be prepared for a negative response.* Ideally, your partner will listen to your pain caused by his or her Internet addiction, accept your perspective, engage in a productive discussion, and agree to concrete changes. It's also possible that no matter how specific and nonblaming you are, your partner will keep attacking, defending, mocking, and counterblaming you, and running back to the computer corner. You are dealing with addiction, don't forget. This is the most challenging and pivotal moment

you're likely to face. If you recoil and don't speak up again, your partner's behavior won't change and you'll feel even worse.

Stay true to your needs, and stick with your goals. Don't engage your partner in a lengthy argument. If it's clear that he or she is not willing to communicate openly this time, suspend your efforts and walk away. But try again the next day or the next week, using the same strategies I've outlined. And add your feelings about how you're now increasingly hurt, worried, or frustrated by your partner's refusal to listen.

7. *Consider other alternatives.* If your attempts at communicating in person fail, don't despair. Try writing your partner a letter. Silly as it may sound to write a letter to the person you live with, you may find benefits to a longer forum that allows you to communicate all your thoughts and feelings without interruption from your partner. Reading your letter in a less charged atmosphere may allow your partner to drop a defensive posture and respond to you in a more balanced manner. You might even consider communicating by e-mail, which not only offers the same freedom of interruptions as letters but can demonstrate to your partner that you don't view the Internet itself as entirely evil. You both might even share a laugh at the irony of taking this approach, which could open the door to a more productive face-to-face talk.

You also might consider requesting couples counseling, preferably with a therapist who understands the Internet and its particular allure. In counseling, you may get to the heart of your message more quickly and easily and work your way to the roots of your marital discord. Perhaps your partner found your sex life uninspiring and turned to cybersex for passion and adventure. Once your feelings have been heard and steps taken to address them, you might engage in ways to open to your more passionate side.

As a final alternative, especially if your partner refuses to join you in couples counseling, seek out the support of a counselor by yourself. A trained professional can help supply the validation you didn't get from your partner and assist you in weighing your options. If you tune in to what you need and act accordingly, you no longer are a victim, even if you choose to end the relationship.

## CYBERLOVERS: ADDICTS OR CHEATERS?

It's tempting to condemn any married person like David for betraying a spouse through a cyberaffair or even just secretive cybersex. Sure, intimacy grips a potential on-line wanderer more quickly than any real-life encounter, where social constraints and physical and verbal cues often tend to dilute raw passions and reckless behavior. Yes, erotic dialogue may seem harmless when it's simply words on a computer, even if both partners are in a committed relationship with other people. But in the cold light of day, it's easy to take a hard-line attitude that says the on-line wanderer should know better. My own compassion and professional understanding of the addiction behind the deviant behavior occasionally gets tested, as it did when I received this e-mail:

> *Read your article on Internet addiction . . . took the quiz . . . got the worst possible score . . . but know what, don't really care . . . Yes, I am TOTALLY addicted but having best time of my life . . . I'm mother of two kids, 13 and 11 . . . used to be very devoted, but now I live for the Internet . . . I hide a lot of dirty laundry, make quickest meals possible . . . could go on and on . . . on-line loves? met a few . . . even planning a vacation with one . . . everyone in my family is worried sick . . . my husband is ready to throw the computer out the window . . . poor guy, he's suffering . . . gotta go . . . Bye--Paula.*

It's difficult to understand or to empathize with Paula, but it's important to remember that something in her life had propelled her toward Internet addiction and its destructive consequences. I never heard from her again to learn what it was. But another day I got a call from Matthew, a young stockbroker in Florida who was married and had a baby daughter. He admitted he had progressed from a few casual cyberflings to actual meetings with three women from the steamy on-line meeting rooms.

"In the back of my mind, my marriage vows disappeared," Matthew began. "I just let the thoughts of how good the sex was with these women on the computer, and how much better it would be in person, take over my conscience. I lied to my wife three times about having to go on business trips so I could be with these other women."

On the phone with me, Matthew poured out intense feelings of guilt, remorse, and fear. How could he have done this, he asked himself. Would he be able to stop himself next time? Had he become a perverted sex addict? In talking to him briefly, I learned that both Matthew and his wife had grown up strict Catholics, with rigid guidelines about appropriate and acceptable sexual behavior even for married men and women. On some level, Matthew resented the rigidity and longed to act out his repressed desires. Cybersex unleashed those desires, and he quickly lost control.

I urged Matthew to find a therapist to talk about his experiences and explore his jumbled feelings and impulses. For the short term, I also advised him to cease all contact with women on the Internet. Once he had regained control and gathered some understanding of his addiction and its triggers, of course, he would need to tell his wife what he had done and ask for her forgiveness. Through couples counseling, they may be able to repair the damages and rebuild their relationship on a more honest foundation.

Anne, however, had lost that option. Married for 17 years to a husband who worked until late at night, she filled her loneliness and sexual frustration with hours of cyberporn and cybersex. With one cybersex partner in England, she even videotaped herself in action during one of their intense on-line encounters and mailed him the evidence. That inspired a real-life, nine-day rendezvous and talk of living together in England. Anne's husband found out and immediately filed for divorce.

"We had been arguing about my computer use before, but I just thought my husband was being a jerk. We had problems earlier in the marriage and I just saw the computer as one more thing for him to complain about. I never considered that I was the one with the problem," Anne lamented. "It wasn't until I got the divorce papers served to me that I realized I had completely ignored our marriage because of the on-line world I discovered. That's when I knew I was really addicted."

Not surprisingly, Anne's romance with Buzz, the nine-day wonder, ended after that first visit. In the heat of their sexual intensity Buzz had left out a few details of his life, including the fact that he was unemployed and recently had been convicted of burglary. Alone for the first time in her adult life, Anne told me she wanted to understand what had happened to her and chart a new course. With her motivation and determination, and by following some of the recovery strategies of the previous chapters, Anne stood a solid chance of rebounding from her crisis and moving on more calmly and wisely.

But when Anne contacted me, she symbolized the wandering partner left trying to dig out of the same kind of rubble that cyberwidows find themselves under when terminal love hits them with tornado force. When terminal love strikes committed relationships, few escape unscathed.

# SIX

# Parents, Kids, and a Technological Time Bomb

*Eighty-six percent of responding teachers, librarians, and computer coordinators believe that Internet usage by children does not improve classroom performance.*
—SURVEY REPORTED BY USA TODAY

The Internet has emerged as a popular educational tool for children so rapidly and dramatically that most parents don't know what to make of it all. Unable to keep up with all the new and conflicting information about what the Net really is, how it works, and what it can and can't do for their children, parents tend to fall quickly into one of two extreme response modes: benign neglect or outright banishment.

Judging from the many teenagers who regard me as their on-line confidante for Internet-related problems, I'd say the first response is far more prevalent. Parents, these teens tell me, are clueless about what their kids do on the Internet and don't seem to care.

"Everyone says that kids need to learn to use this new computer technology," these parents tell themselves. "They've got them in the schools now, so I should get Jenny her own personal computer and modem for her bedroom so she can practice at home. She's got to keep up with the other kids."

If parents don't even know how to turn on a computer themselves, they're in the dark about the workings of the Internet and how their children are adjusting to it. But, they figure, whatever they're up to, it's sure better than wasting all their time watching television, because the Internet is supposed to be educational. So parents don't get involved, don't ask children many questions, don't monitor their on-line time and activities. They shrug their shoulders and say to themselves: "My kid knows more about the Internet than I do."

But some parents have gone to the opposite extreme by banning the Internet from their homes entirely. They're terrified of this new "demon" that threatens their children's safety and well-being. "I've heard about the kooks and weirdos out there in that computer world and what they can do to kids," they say. "My child is not going anywhere near this stuff." These parents are reacting to some of the more sensational stories in the media:

- A 13-year-old girl in New Hampshire gets chummy with a boy who tells her on-line that he's 16 and invites her to meet in person, where she learns he's really 22. The girls' parents find out about this secret liaison and cut off her on-line account. In this modern-day Romeo and Juliet story, the forbidden young lovers run away together and are found only through a nationwide hunt.

- A 12-year-old boy in Missouri runs up a $1,200 phone bill dialing Internet access in another city so he can tap into adult, late-night chat rooms. When his mother gets the bill, she severs his Internet connection and takes him to see a juvenile officer. That same night, police say, the boy shoots and kills his mother and himself.

- A task force on electronic commerce appointed by President Clinton reveals that businesses advertising on the World Wide Web routinely lure kids into volunteering their real names, addresses, and phone numbers in exchange for gifts of T-shirts and CD players. Not only is such personal information used for unwanted Internet marketing aimed directly at young kids, but many companies sell the names to others, leaving data on these cybertots circulating throughout the unregulated Web.

- A lawsuit against America Online is filed on behalf of a 14-year-old boy who was sexually assaulted by a man he met in an AOL chat room. A Florida state judge rules that America Online is not liable for customers who become cyberspace pedophiles and declares that responsibility for protecting children against unwanted on-line advances rests squarely with parents.

- A Cleveland man is arrested by federal authorities and accused of using the Internet to entice teenagers to make sex videos of themselves and send them to him. Several teens and preteens had sent such videos to this man, who allegedly claimed on-line to be 15 years old when he was really 47.

Neither blinding yourself to your child's Internet use or prohibiting it completely will help parents of teens and preteens effectively confront the important issues the Internet raises for families today. By practicing benign neglect, you leave your child vulnerable to the very real problems and dangers lurking in the on-line underworld. When you miss the warning signs that your child may be getting hooked on this new technology that you don't understand, you risk hastening the same kinds of addictive complications that plague adult Internet addicts.

Banishing the Internet from the home, however, deprives children and their parents of opportunities for new and exciting experiences and even a potential shared learning together. By taking this posture, you are naively suggesting that children can be shielded from the temptations of the Internet indefinitely, which is akin to believing that your child can be protected from all threats of drugs and violence in our schools and streets.

The real challenge for parents, then, is to tune in to what the Internet is all about so they can actively engage in directing its proper role in their children's lives. By gaining a better understanding of how kids are using the Internet and the legitimate concerns of the free-flowing cyberspace environment, parents can emerge well informed and wisely cautious.

So if you're a parent whose child already has begun using the Internet or likely will be exposed to it soon, pay close attention to the examples of children and parents that we're about to explore. Learn the warning signs of Internet addiction for children, and if you determine that your child is already hooked, make use of my age-appropriate recovery strategies. We'll also look at ways to deal with those real dangers that await an unknowing child navigating the Internet. And we'll compare the current and potential impact of the Internet on family life with the influence of that more familiar demon—television.

## FROM INNOCENCE TO CRISIS

It seemed harmless in the beginning, Martha told me. When her husband, Jim, bought a new computer for himself, he gave his old one to their two sons. Timothy, 15, and Peter, 13. Timothy played computer games now and then, but he was finding more exciting adolescent endeavors outside home. Peter, who always had been a bit more introverted than his brother, immediately took to surfing the Web. Then a friend pointed him to e-mail and the two communicated with each other for hours after school. Soon they wandered into the chat rooms.

Martha knew something about computers from her work as a travel agent. She even watched over Peter's shoulders the first week or two. She didn't understand all the chat-room lingo, so her son had to explain that BRB meant "be right back" and lol translated into "laugh out loud." She thought it quaint that teenagers were developing their own computer language and she was encouraged to see her shy son reaching out in a social environment. So she stopped standing guard.

It didn't take long for problems to manifest. First, Peter had more trouble getting up for school in the morning. Then Martha noticed he was spending more time alone in his room, seldom even venturing out for his favorite TV shows. On his next report card, Peter, a consistent A and B student, brought home one B and three Cs. Martha and her husband asked Peter if anything was wrong, but he said everything was great and he was having more fun than he used to.

Though concerned, Martha at first let the matter rest. She figured he's in puberty, he's adjusting to his new middle school, maybe this is a normal phase that will pass. Jim strongly believed in new technology and couldn't imagine the Internet as a problem. He was more pleased at Peter's brighter attitude than upset about the grades. But then Jim and Martha got their next phone bill showing more than $1,000 worth of long-distance calls to Ohio, Colorado, Florida, and even England. Peter had been calling his chat-room friends from all over the world!

Martha and Jim confronted Peter and told him he could use the computer only when they were with him. He rebelled by yelling at them and throwing his things against his bedroom wall. They took the phone line out of his room so he couldn't use the modem. That solved the problem, they thought. Then they got the next phone bill, and it was higher than the previous one. Peter, it turns out, had bought his own phone cord and wired it out his bedroom window to the outside phone jack in a desperate attempt to maintain his Internet usage and follow-up phone chats.

Not used to such displays of disobedience and defiance from Peter, his parents punished him by grounding him for a month and removing his computer from his room and hiding it in a closet. Enraged, Peter grabbed a hammer while his parents were at work and smashed his father's new computer to pieces. At this point, the family entered counseling.

"Even then we didn't realize that it was his computer usage itself that was causing the problems in his behavior," Martha relates. "We knew he had a problem, but we kept looking for something else. We never even talked about his activities while he was using the Internet, and we had no idea that his usage had increased as much as it had. We just thought he was angry and rebellious."

For almost a year, the family floundered. They didn't connect with their counselor. Sometimes when Peter threw a tantrum, they caved in and allowed him some Internet time in hopes of achieving peace. Or when his behavior calmed down, they offered him limited hours on the computer as a reward, only to find Peter deviously staying up all night on-line and falling asleep in school. So they took the computer away again and hired a home tutor, whom Peter alternately yelled at or ignored. Now even more desperate, Martha and Jim went with Peter to a crisis intervention center for families.

At last, they found help. The therapist there talked to Peter about just how much he had been using the computer, what he did there, and how it made him feel. She also asked how Peter felt when his parents deprived him of the Internet. From Peter's responses, she recognized that Peter had become obsessed with the Internet and depended on the social contact he had discovered there. And his acting out against his parents and tutor could at least partially be attributed to the anger, irritability, and edginess he experienced from having his supply of social contact cut off—the cybershakes.

Equally important, the therapist helped the family understand how Peter's excessive Internet use was prompted by low self-esteem. She worked with him alone on that issue, and in family therapy Jim and Martha learned how to provide Peter with more of the attention, acceptance, and validation he craved from them. Once he felt better about himself, Peter was able to enjoy other social outlets. The therapist also helped Peter's parents adopt realistic goals for his Internet usage without forcing Peter to quit cold turkey.

Within months, Peter had cut his Internet time down by about two-thirds and spent part of his remaining on-line hours with his father. He even met a girl whom he soon took out on escorted dates to movies and skating rinks. Martha read everything she could find about the Internet and did some on-line exploring of her own, so she could understand more clearly what had drawn Peter to it so strongly and alert other parents at school to what could happen. When she spoke to me during my Internet addiction study, she hoped she could convince other parents to watch how the Internet was affecting their child's life from the start.

## RECOVERY STRATEGY 12:
### *Watch for Children's Warning Signs*

Many parents at least ask their children how much time they're spending on the Internet. But many kids are apt to lie, especially if they're already addicted. If the computer is in their room, you have no way of knowing the truth. But if you watch their behavior for the following warning signs, you can begin to ascertain whether your child's Internet use has progressed to overuse.

■ *Excessive fatigue.* Does your child struggle to get up in the morning more than he or she did before the computer came along? Do you see signs of drowsiness at dinner and on weekends? As with adults, change in sleep patterns for children often represents the first indicator of excessive on-line time.

■ *Academic problems.* This is where parents get tripped up easily. When their child's grades slip, the last culprit they suspect is the computer; they believe that when their son or daughter is typing away they're diligently working on their homework or writing papers. More likely, they're frittering away hours chatting instead of studying.

■ *Declining interest in hobbies.* After latching on to the Internet, one boy who once referred to making Eagle Scout as his main goal in life suddenly quit Scouts and called it boring. Other kids lose interest in band practice, the yearbook, drama club, or sports. The Internet, for them, has become more than a new hobby—it's an obsession that renders all other activities meaningless.

■ *Withdrawal from friends.* "My daughter is dating a young man in Germany," a mother told me. Only on the Internet, of course. Whether previously shy like Peter or outgoing and popular at school, a child getting caught in the Net often refuses to go to the mall, parties, movies, or anywhere else to be with other kids. As these children form emotional attachments to their cyberbro or cybersis, they become increasingly distant and uncommunicative with their family.

■ *Disobedience and acting out.* When parents first question their child about his or her Internet use, they're likely to be met with anger and hostility. "I'm just having fun!" the child screams and may throw tantrums to protest interference. If parents set rules, the child may well break them, often with the kind of sneaky acts we saw in Peter. And if they take away the computer, the child gets more angry and belligerent; withdrawal is especially disorienting to a child less accustomed to radical mood shifts.

If your child demonstrates three or more of these warning signs, he or she may be addicted to the Internet. Teens or even preteens can become just as psychologically dependent on the Internet's interactive features as the adults we've seen in the previous chapters. Kids get hooked on the on-line socializing and games as a means to feel better about themselves and avoid the stresses of school, adolescence, and family life. But before you rush in to intervene, take some time to consider other factors and problems that may be contributing to the behavior.

First, recognize that these warning signs of addiction may apply to alcoholism or drug use. It's possible that your child is abusing a substance rather than the Internet. Keep this in mind when you approach him or her. Also, remember that as we saw with the profile of an onlineaholic, other psychological problems may be contributing to the added allure of the Internet. A child may be depressed about school or social struggles and turn to the Net as a safe, nonthreatening escape. An anxious child may be temporarily calmed by the easy acceptance and camaraderie among his or her Net pals. That calming state becomes more attractive with more Internet time.

In dealing with the Internet and children, parents also should consider the possible involvement of Attention

Deficit Disorder. A child who has trouble learning because of inattention, disorganization, and being easily distracted and fidgety may gravitate to the Internet because of the rapidly moving and changing material online. The kaleidoscope of dazzling colors and pictures, information bits, and mindless chatter may enable a child with ADD to sit at a computer for hours at a time more comfortably than trying to read school books.

Finally, remember that children falling into any addictive pattern may be doing so as a cry for help—not just for their own problems but for a larger issue involving their family. That son or daughter hiding away for hours on the computer and lapsing into sleep deprivation, poor grades, and social withdrawal may be what family therapists call the "identified patient," a kind of scapegoat for a family in distress. Internet addiction may be a by-product of Mom's alcoholism, Dad's workaholism, or the family's unresolved and unaddressed grief over Grandma's death. Use this opportunity to take your own inventory of possible underlying family problems before focusing all attention on your child and the Internet.

## RECOVERY STRATEGY 13:
### *Intervening with Addicted Children*

Once you've determined that you need to approach your child about his or her Internet use, you'll be practicing many of the same steps outlined in Strategy 11, Follow the Seven Steps of Communication, in the previous chapter. Just as you would in confronting a spouse, you want to be clear about your goals with your child and wait for a quiet, nonstressful time to talk. You need to decide what you want to say, use nonblaming language, and listen empathetically to your child's response. But the challenges of communicating with children about Internet addiction—or almost any sensitive issue—require special skills and considerations:

■ *Present a united front.* In a two-parent household, it's critical that both parents take the issue seriously and agree on common goals. If your partner initially seems less open to regarding the Internet as a real problem, use this book to discuss the situation together and help broaden his or her perspective. If necessary, compromise on your desired goals so that when you approach your child, you'll be on the same page. If you don't, your child will appeal to the more skeptical parent and create division between you.

■ *Show your caring.* It will help to begin your discussion by reminding your child that you love him or her and that you care about his or her happiness and well-being. Children often interpret any question about their behavior as blaming and criticism. You need to reassure your child that you're not saying he or she is wrong. Rather, tell your child you're concerned about some of the changes you've seen and refer to those changes in specific terms: fatigue, declining grades, giving up hobbies, social withdrawal.

■ *Assign an Internet time log.* Tell your child that you'd like to see an accounting of just how much time he or she spends on-line each day and which Internet activities the child engages in. Remind your child that with television you can monitor viewing habits more easily, but with the Internet you need his or her help and cooperation to become appropriately involved. Put your child on the honor system to keep the log for a week or two to build trust between you. If they balk at this idea or clearly lie in their log, you're likely dealing with their denial of addiction.

■ *Set reasonable rules.* **Many parents get angry when they see the signs of Internet addiction in their child and take the computer away as a form of punishment. Others become frightened and force their child to quit cold turkey, believing that's the only way to get rid of the problem. Both approaches invite trouble—your child will internalize the message that they're bad; they'll look at you as the enemy instead of an ally; and they'll suffer real withdrawal symptoms of nervousness, anger, and irritability. Instead, work with your child to establish clear boundaries of limited Internet usage. Perhaps an hour per night after homework will fit, with a few extra weekend hours. Stick to your rules and remember that you're not simply trying to control your child, you're working to free him or her of a psychological dependence.**

■ *Make the computer visible.* **At least for the short term, move the child's personal computer out of the bedroom and into the more visible kitchen or dining area. You don't want to stare over your child's shoulder every minute he or she is on-line, but by walking by now and then in your normal home activities you send the message that the Internet is not something the child can use on the sly. As you'll recall, an insistence on privacy for Internet time usually indicates that the user is doing something he or she wants to hide. If your child needs privacy to write a paper on the computer, allow him or her to move it back to the bedroom temporarily. But keep the modem in your possession so you'll know when the child go on-line.**

■ *Encourage other activities.* **When you cut down your child's Internet time, he or she will be looking for something to do, not only to fill in the hours but to achieve a comparable "high." Help children find alternative endeavors, whether it be something they used to enjoy or** something new, like a chess club at school. Talk to your child about what he or she most enjoys on the Net so you can steer him or her toward a healthy alternative. If your child especially enjoyed taking on many different handles on-line and acting in the character of those different personalities, encourage him or her to go out for the school play. And remind children that they still can have the same fun on the Internet, only within limits.

■ *Support, don't enable.* Just as with spouses, parents often fall into an enabling role with an Internet-addicted child. They cover up or make excuses for their children when they miss school or fail to meet deadlines, and in the name of keeping peace they give in to their children's demands when they complain loudly. If your child does rebel against your intervention efforts, let the first storm subside. Acknowledge your child's feelings—it must not be easy to feel that you're tugging at his or her only lifeline—but stick to your goals. Validate your child for any effort he or she is making to work with you. Remind your child that other kids have had problems with the Internet and that they found a new way, and that you support your child in making these difficult changes.

■ *Use outside resources when needed.* If your child is unable to moderate his or her Internet usage and the initial problems persist, along with new hostility in your relationship with them, it's best to seek outside help. After reading this book, you might visit a local alcohol and drug treatment program to gather more information about addictions. As a parent, you might gain support for your own feelings by attending an Alanon meeting. Hopefully, your concerns will be taken seriously, but even if you just listen, you'll be comforted by hearing other parents' struggles in dealing with their children's addiction to other substances or activities. School counselors can help alert you to your child's behavior at school. Ultimately, family therapy may be your best bet to help guide your child's recovery, address family strife, and heal wounds old and new.

## TEENAGERS IN SEARCH OF A CONFIDANT

Dozens of teenagers have contacted me on-line to tell me that they knew or feared that they had a problem with the Internet. I appreciated the opportunity to provide them information, listen to their stories, and offer suggestions for moderating their usage. But when I urged them to take their concerns to their parents or other trusted adults in their immediate circle, they shared their deep frustration and distrust of adults who know little or nothing about the Internet and its special appeal. Even when I reassured these teens in distress that they could refer their parents to me to help educate them about Internet addiction, they usually rejected my suggestion.

I noticed a similar on-line response to a short article in *Seventeen* magazine inviting "Web girls" with a dependency on the Internet to seek tips for quitting in an on-line recovery circle. A large influx of teenage girls immediately responded, confessing to their Internet obsessions and bemoaning their parents' lack of understanding about the mystery and allure of the on-line world.

I understood these teenagers' predicament. Approaching a parent about Internet addiction is even more intimidating than talking to them about abusing drugs or alcohol, something they're apt to know much more about and may well have experienced in their own lives or at least witnessed in a friend or loved one. Just as many teenagers have pushed well ahead of their parents in terms of understanding what the Internet is and how to use it, they're also much more acquainted with the Internet's potential downside.

Parents have some catching up to do. Even before a child slides into an addiction to the Internet and displays the warning signs we've discussed, parents need to know more about the workings of the Internet and its allure to teenagers. To begin, let's visit the world of Mark, a 13-year-old from Puerto Rico who turns to the Internet's interactive games not only for fun and stimulation but also to find answers to real-life questions and problems.

Mark is home-schooled, which means that when he's not directly engaged in his lessons for the day he has ready access to the Net. He spends most of his on-line time in Mirkwood, a typical MUD. His character is Branagan, a shade thief. He chose this identity because he finds it both evil and intelligent. Like most MUDs, Mirkwood is an active game, and Mark has done his share of killing creatures and leveling obstacles. But after awhile he finds such activities boring. He now prefers to hang out in the Tribe Commons Room seeking counsel from "VanillaFudge," a fellow Mirkwood player whom Mark believes is in his 20s. Here's a typical conversation between VanillaFudge and Branagan during one MUD session. Notice how MUDders use words to describe their own physical responses.

> VANILLAFUDGE: *So, you were saying 'bout life . . .*
> BRANAGAN: *It just seems needlessly complex for something that doesn't even amount to anything in the end.*
> VANILLAFUDGE NODS.
> BRANAGAN: *I've been feeling this great sense of urgency.*
> VANILLAFUDGE: *To do what?*
> BRANAGAN: *Everything . . . sigh . . . feels as though if I don't do it now, I'll never get a chance to do it (it being the things I \*want\* to do, not need to.) What do you think?*

*VANILLAFUDGE SHUFFLES HIS FEET AND BLUSHES:* Well, I'm
   bombing psychology, so don't expect a sure-fire opinion.
*BRANAGAN ROLLS ON THE FLOOR, LAUGHING HYSTERICALLY.*
*VANILLAFUDGE:* But I dunno, Bill Cosby can prob'ly sum it up
   best when he says there's always time for Jello.
*BRANAGAN:* Well, I'll think about it. Normally, I think about
   things too much. Hey, I need yer opinion on another
   thing.
*VANILLAFUDGE:* Sure, what?
*BRANAGAN:* I've got long hair . . . it's about to my elbows,
   and I want to get it in dreadlocks . . . my mom and 2 sis-
   ters both support me in this, BUT . . .
*VANILLAFUDGE:* Dad?
*BRANAGAN:* Completely opposed to it . . . so, should I just do it
   or try to convert him or just forget it?
*VANILLAFUDGE:* Try and convert.
*BRANAGAN:* When I try, he just says it may be my business but
   he has to be with me around people.
*VANILLAFUDGE:* So what would happen if you just went home
   with it one day?
*BRANAGAN:* I guess the worst thing he could do is make me
   shave 'em off, and leave me bald.
*VANILLAFUDGE SNICKERS:* Then tell him dreadlocks increase
   thinking power on tests.
*BRANAGAN LICKS HIS MOUTH AND SMILES.*

## IN THEIR OWN WORDS

When I interviewed Mark on-line, he admitted to spending as many as nine hours every day in such conversations
with VanillaFudge, a person he never sees or talks to in
real-life. Mark clearly is escaping from life around him,
and when I spoke to him I began to zero in on the likely
explanation. I'll share an excerpt from that interview so

you can see how one adolescent Internet user expresses himself on-line:

DR. YOUNG: *How do you feel when you're playing a MUD? Are these new feelings for you?*

MARK: *It kinda wakes me up, and i feel exhilarated and get really happy and excited: not really new feelings, but i didn't used to feel them very often.*

DR. YOUNG: *What was your life like before MUDding? Has it changed, and if so, how?*

MARK: *Before i started mudding my interaction with computers was a few e-mails a week and solitaire . . . for some reason, when i started mudding i got more interested in all aspects of computers, and i investigated everything about them . . . now i sleep 'bout four hours a night.*

DR. YOUNG: *What was your relationship with your parents like before, and how is it now?*

MARK: *well, hmmm . . . lemme explain . . . for awhile now there's been a lot of conflict between my mom/dad, fights, etc . . . i avoid my mom/dad because i just can't handle the tension around them . . . they tend to blow up at anything you say/do. Unless they're not around each other, then they act totally different. my mom doesn't see me much, but she knows i spend a lot of time on the computer . . . every now and then she makes a comment that "my head will turn into a monitor" but that's about it.*

DR. YOUNG: *I don't mean to intrude on you and your privacy, but I was wondering if either of your parents would be willing to talk with me, either via e-mail or by phone-- phone might be easier for them. Please let me know how comfortable you are with this. I'd like to study how MUDs affect the whole family, so any help you could be would be appreciated.*

MARK: *well, they probably would be willing, but i'm not really comfortable with that . . . i'm not exactly, ah, completely truthful when it comes down to the details of mudding*

*with my parents. if they knew i got 4 hours of sleep when
i said i had 9, they probably wouldn't let me mud anymore.*

Part of the reason Mark had become obsessively involved with the Internet is to avoid the stress of his parents' struggling relationship. If he told them about his
addictive behavior, he risked being blamed and shut off
from the only outlet for his distress. Mark could well have
been placed in the role of the identified patient we discussed earlier; his parents would focus their attention on
his Internet problem without recognizing how their marital distress contributed to it. He and his parents needed
family counseling to understand these dynamics and help
mend their relationships so Mark once again could trust
his parents to confide in.

Even preteens turn to Internet pals for friendship and
confidants, sharing feelings and secrets their parents
never know. Kidscom, an educational Web page, invites
kids to play games, do logic puzzles, and learn about new
activities. "Graffiti Walls," a Kidscom feature that's sort of
a chat room for children, allows kids to type notes that
appear on the wall for all to see. On the first line of the
message, kids fill in their on-line handle, age, gender, interests, and hobbies. On the second line, they type a
statement to the group. The program has separate divisions for children ages 11 and over, and 11 and under.
Here's an excerpt from the younger group:

WeeZee/11/m/love Nirvana and sports
*I just spent two boring days with my dad. Ho hum*
Mocha/f/11/love talkin on the phone/love music
*How is the food at your school cafeteria, Tweety? Mine sucks*
Blue Dragon/m/11/bh/be/all sports/taken by lolpop/
*Your dad sounds like my grandparents, WeeZee. Spent the
whole weekend with them, pretty boring*

Tweety/*12/f/c-sis Silver Tab*
*Food sucks here too. Got a project for school. gotta go do homework*
Crystal/*11/f/love sports/running/alternative music*
*I am so depressed, my c-bro hasn't been on all week*
Tweety
*Don't cry over him, Crystal. Just dump him and find another. They come and they go. Take it from me.*
Jonathan/*12/m*
*I have blonde hair, blue eyes, and like alternative. I'll be your c-bro if you want. My e-mail address is _____*
Crystal
*Thanks, Jonathan. I would like that, my e-mail address is*

_____

## A BIG CITY WITH NO POLICE

That Graffiti Walls excerpt may have sounded like harmless childhood chatter, but an alert parent educated in the ways of the Internet would spot the potential dangers. First, though the group supposedly was limited to kids 11 and under, some kids listed their age as 12. And as we know, Internet users young and old lie about their age on-line. Rather than 12, Jonathan might well have been 32. His quick move to volunteer his private e-mail address to the distressed Crystal might have been an innocent gesture between two kids, or it could have been an adult's first move in establishing trust with a child that would pave the way for later invitations to talk on the phone, exchange sexually explicit photos, or even offer the child a gift in return for meeting in person.

Pedophiles tend to lurk around those chat rooms restricted to children, looking for kids who feel isolated and dejected. They show understanding and support and win the child's favor by offering to be their "special" friend. Even when the children themselves wonder if this special friend is exactly who they say they are, they figure it's not real because it's happening in the safe and anonymous computer world. It's not like a stranger pulling up beside them in a car and offering to give them a ride home. And when this computer friend invites them to talk on the phone, children often feel they can't disappoint their new pal or they'll lose this special status and maybe even jeopardize their popularity in this virtual hangout. Anyway, no one but the two of them knows what's going on.

"This (cyberspace) is like a giant city with no police force," a police officer in Lancaster, Pennsylvania, concluded. Law enforcement officials have begun to go undercover posing as children to catch pedophiles in the act. To test the prevalence of such deviant on-line behavior, I entered a general chat room posing as Marcie, a 15-year-old girl. Within minutes, a man who said he was 40 approached me. "I understand how difficult it is to live with parents," he said. "I am much more supportive than your parents."

Even if they're never subjected to unwanted advances to meet or talk on the phone with ill-intentioned adults, children can be exposed to sexually oriented material in many forums. Most children can wander into the lobbies, or meeting grounds, of adult chat rooms. In a recent visit to one such lobby, I noticed these messages that children also could be viewing: "Anyone looking for hot chat?" "Looking for hot pictures?" "Lonely and very willing if anyone is interested." Several on-line systems now promote parental control features that deny access to the private and sexually explicit rooms where anyone answering provocative chat-room messages would be led. But as a 14-year-old boy lamented: "Being in the general chat areas is like sitting in a bar watching two people have sex in public."

Children also could land in Romance Connection, where I recently received an e-mail from a man that included a picture to download. Before I realized it, I was staring at a sexually explicit picture of two men and a woman. On the Net, few places are safe for children. Even on the World Wide Web, cyberporn is readily accessible to children. Some graphic sites carry the warning "No one under 18 permitted to enter" across the screen. If you click on the site, you are asked: "Are you at least 18 years of age?" A simple click of the yes button ushers you into a lobby teeming with XXX videos, nude pictures, and phone numbers for sex talk. Unlike an X-rated bookstore, no real person is checking for IDs.

Alarmed by the availability of so many sexually oriented Internet offerings, many parents have urged tighter on-line restrictions and government regulations, such as the 1996 Communications Decency Act, which made it a crime to transmit indecent material over the Internet in a manner available to minors. But Internet operators, backed by those who say such a law violates free speech rights, fought to have the law overturned. They argued that the Internet should be self-regulated. In June 1997 the Supreme Court unanimously struck down the Communications Decency Act, once again leaving ultimate responsibility of protecting Internet-active children in the hands of parents.

It's a daunting task. Even with those programs that screen out the more obvious and blatant inappropriate material for children, adult language often surfaces in even the most benign-appearing Internet locales. One mother was sitting with her seven-year-old daughter looking at a Web site established by Troll Communications, which sells books to elementary school students. When they visited "Flying to Planet Troll," mother and daughter were greeted with this riddle: "Why did the Vampire go into the cave?" It sounded educational to this mom, so she helped her daughter enter a response, which appeared on screen with a hundred previous answers that included: "To have sex" and "shut the f___ up."

"Mommy," the second grader asked her mother, "what does it mean to have sex?"

## TAKING A PROACTIVE PARENTAL RESPONSE

No matter how old your child is, you need to get on the Internet and see for yourself what's out there. With television, parents can watch a program to get an idea of the content their children are exposed to, so don't they want the same knowledge of their children's favorite Internet activities? Ask your child what he or she does on-line, and get a sample of a typical session in a MUD or chat room. Parents need to talk openly to children about the dangers of the Internet, just as they might discuss alcohol or drug use. Have they heard some of these stories about pedophiles? Do they think adults really pose as kids on-line with deviant intentions, and do other kids at their school talk about this? Have they come across a business offering gifts in exchange for their name, address, and phone number, and if so, did they ever volunteer their own personal information?

As parents educate themselves and their children about the dangers on-line, they should make sure they give equal time to the benefits. Ask children what they most enjoy about the Internet and validate them for appropriate ways they've found to have fun, build confidence, and expand their horizons on the Net. Urge them to share what they've learned in their Web surfing about geography or other cultures. Get them to describe what they liked about Web sites they consider especially creative or engaging. If they like to chat on-line, whom are they meeting, where do they live, and how do these friends' lives compare with their own? If they prefer the interactive games, do they go for the aggressive action or the friendly bantering among players?

With teenagers especially, you don't want to demonize the Internet. To a teen, that puts you in the same category as a parent who criticizes all alternative music or off-beat hairstyles or clothing. You don't want to deny them a freedom before they've abused it, nor should you be governed by your distrust before you've allowed them to win your trust over how much they use the Internet and what they do on it. If you haven't spotted the warning signs of addiction we've discussed in their behavior, cut them some slack. Give them a chance to exercise personal responsibility, but encourage and maintain an open dialogue about the Internet so it doesn't become an unknown, private world. More important, if your teenager does encounter a problem, he or she will feel safe to approach you about it.

## RECOVERY STRATEGY 14:
### *Teach Young Kids the Do's and Don'ts*

For preteens or early adolescents, it's wise to get more directly involved. If your child has just been introduced to the Internet at school, learn about what he or she is doing there, and if you have on-line access at home, sit down at the computer and explore cyberspace with your child. Not only will this give you greater control over your child's Internet experience, it also will provide you a chance to share an activity together. If parents have e-mail access, they can send children messages and follow up with them to see if they received them. If you come across something on the Web that you know your child would enjoy, show it to him or her. Make it a new adventure, but a safe one. When children begin to spend on-line time alone, guard against the dangers that await them by teaching them these basic do's and don'ts:

*DO'S*

■ Do log off immediately and tell your parent (or another trusted adult) if anyone says something to you on the Internet that makes you uncomfortable or asks you to do something that you know is wrong. If possible, write down the person's on-line handle so an adult can follow up.

■ Do log off and inform a parent if that same person tries to contact you again.

■ Do log off and inform a parent if someone sends you sexually explicit pictures electronically.

■ Do inform a parent if you come across any bad language or sexually oriented content, even if it's not directed at you individually.

*DON'TS*

■ Don't give out your full name, phone number, address, or any other personal information you wouldn't share with a stranger.

■ Don't accept gifts from anyone you meet on-line.

■ Don't call anyone you encounter on the Internet on the phone, even if the other person invites you to call them collect.

■ Don't enter any Web site or room where you see a warning indicating that no one under 18 is allowed.

If your child is faced with one of these experiences and reports it appropriately, praise him or her for doing the right thing. Recognize that young children often feel it's their fault if someone talks dirty to them or makes an unwanted advance. Reassure them that you're not angry with them, that it's not their fault. Remind them that not all people are bad, but there are some people who do inappropriate things on the Internet that they should watch out for, just as they would beware of strangers calling on the phone, ringing the doorbell, or stopping them on the street.

## THE INTERNET: TV OF THE NEXT MILLENNIUM?

Remember when television first became commonplace in the home, accompanied by idyllic images of families gathered in the same room sharing the warmth and discovery of a wholesome movie or *The Wonderful World of Disney*? TV, we were told, would only bring the family together. Flash forward to today: separate TV sets in almost every bedroom, *Sesame Street* and cartoons for the younger kids, MTV for preteens and teens, ESPN for Dad, soap operas and *Oprah* for Mom. If the family ever gathers around one TV in the evening, it's usually to gawk at prime-time displays of sex, crime, violence, and mindless sitcoms.

For many working parents, TV has become an all-too-easy baby-sitter for children. When Dad's on a long phone call or working on a remodeling project, or when the kids get home from school at 3 P.M. and Mom won't be back from work until 6, the instructions to kids are simple: Park yourself in front of the TV and stay out of trouble. Also, instead of spending hours reading or playing active games with their children, many parents have become all too willing to hand the educational chores over to Big Bird.

Rather than bringing the family together, critics say TV has done the opposite. In her book *The Plug-In Drug*, Marie Winn, who studied TV use among children, points out: "In its facilitation of parental withdrawal from an active role in the socialization of their children, and in its replacement of family rituals and special events, television has played an important role in the disintegration of the family."

Is the Internet taking us in the same splintering direction? Will we begin the next century with separate computers and modems in every bedroom, with parents and children forsaking all active communication with one another in favor of impersonal chat-room bantering and slaying imaginary dragons? Will the predicted mass invasion of cyberspace restrict our family contact to e-mail messages reminding Jenny to finish her homework—on the computer, of course—and Jason to cut down those long-distance phone calls to his cyberbro in California?

With the distraction of television, Winn notes that families not only stop meeting at the dinner table, they also use TV "to avoid confronting their problems, problems that will not go away if they are ignored but will only fester and become less resolvable as time goes on." As we've seen, when parents or kids hide behind the computer screen and bury themselves in the Internet, they're not simply avoiding family problems, they're sharing all the private details with strangers! And even if the Internet family occasionally still feels that old yearning to get together and share their common obsession, they can't fit around one computer screen as they might gather to watch one TV.

For children especially, the Internet comes with many of the same features that make TV so addictive and potentially destructive to their growth and development. The information on either screen is passive; the child is not reading a book, constructing a castle with blocks, or creating outdoor games with friends and neighbors. Both TV and the Internet dazzle a child's senses with colorful graphics and rapidly changing images. Children can play video games on either outlet. And for parents considering the Internet as the new permanent baby-sitter, the Internet has a special bonus—it's *quiet!* No more Saturday morning tug-of-wars when you're trying to sleep late and the kids keep turning up the volume on those obnoxious cartoons. Also, you can keep telling yourself that the Internet is educational.

Beyond the similarities, the Internet differs from TV in important ways that make it more of a technological time bomb. As we've seen in this chapter, the Internet's interactive features plunk children down in the middle of steamy streets of an unpoliced city of thousands of anonymous strangers who may, at any click of the mouse, entice them into looking at dirty pictures, invite them to private meetings, pass along their personal information all throughout cyberspace, or even urge them to run away from home.

The Internet also lacks the basic censorship laws and effective parental control devices that TV, for its faults, does offer. While involved parents at least can keep a concerned ear out for the TV programs their children turn to with each click of the remote, Internet surfing is done in silent solitude. Unless parents are right there at the screen, they forfeit their rights to control this selection of programming that comes from hundreds more "channels" than any TV cable. Also, before any TV program ever gets on the air, it must pass the evaluations of network executives who set bottom-line standards of quality and taste. As much as parents may criticize such network quality, no one is making any predetermination of what goes out unedited via the Internet.

## Is It *Really* Educational?

Parents, school administrators, and politicians eager to demonstrate their aggressive support of education all tout the Internet as a primary educational tool for children. Among school systems in the '90s, two definitions became almost as basic as the three Rs:

1.  Computers equal progress.
2.  The Internet equals the cutting edge of progress.

School districts already strapped for money and resources sacrifice other worthy programs and needs in favor of buying computers and hooking up to the Net. States that lag behind in the Internet rush are branded as backward and unresponsive to the needs of children. When President Clinton proclaims the need for every child to be connected to the Internet for the United States to stay competitive in the global marketplace, it not only pressures Americans to get their kids logged on fast, it also spurs competition among other countries to see who can lead the Internet race.

But are kids really benefiting? One U.S. survey revealed that 86 percent of responding teachers, librarians, and computer coordinators believe that Internet usage by children does not improve classroom performance. These voices from inside education determined that information on the Internet is too disorganized and unrelated to school curriculum or textbooks to help students achieve better results on standardized tests.

Schools that can't find a dime for concert choirs or drama clubs fork over millions on sophisticated computer labs without any research into the Internet's general classroom effectiveness or its ability to help students in the real basics of reading, writing, and arithmetic. Also, little consideration is given to related questions such as the cost of training those teachers who are supposed to teach students all about the Internet, and the long-term impact of relinquishing the student-teacher interactive learning model to this impersonal technology.

"Computers are good," the new educational mantra begins, "let's buy them." Then educators shove the Internet into the classroom without even a fraction of the screening and scrutiny that any proposed textbook must pass before it can be placed in the hands of an impressionable child. With the Internet still in its early developmental phase and so many dangers lurking on-line, perhaps it's time for educators to revert back to a much earlier and more basic lesson: Look before you leap.

# SEVEN

# Fraternities of Netheads

*We've put all this money into an educational tool, and some students are using it for self-destruction.*—PROVOST W. RICHARD OTT, ALFRED UNIVERSITY, UPON LEARNING THAT *43%* OF NORMALLY BRIGHT FRESHMEN STUDENTS SURVEYED HAD BEEN DISMISSED DUE TO INTERNET ABUSE

It's after midnight at an upstate New York university, and there's a party on—lots of food and drink, lively conversation, juicy gossip, boyfriends and girlfriends retreating to private corners to pour out their affections. New friendships are forming between students who delight in learning of the many interests and beliefs they share despite coming from separate states or even different countries. The lights stay on at this campus hot spot all night, and by dawn most partygoers slink bleary-eyed back to their dorm rooms. Vampires, some call them. And when darkness descends the next day, they're back. The party cranks up again.

Let's take a closer look at this party, symbolic of what's fast becoming the most popular college activity of the late '90s. While the chips and cookies might resemble the same munchies of parties in decades past, we see that instead of beer, the drink of choice tends to be the nonalcoholic Jolt, selected because of its extra dose of caffeine to keep participants awake and alert. We also notice how this party is eerily quiet—no blaring music, no outrageous dancing, no shouting or singing to keep other students awake or arouse the suspicions of campus security making late-night rounds.

In fact, these party animals seldom leave their seats. No, they're not passing joints around, either. Usually, they don't interact with their fellow partygoers seated beside them at all. That lively conversation, juicy gossip, secret romancing, and new bonds with friends from afar—it's all happening through their individual computer terminals. This is, after all, a gathering of a typical fraternity of netheads, those Internet-obsessed students who every night fill the large computer labs sprinkled throughout campus. Seated in row upon row of terminals all hooked up to the Internet, these busy young men and women are taking advantage of their free and unlimited on-line access—their ticket to one continuous, semester-long party.

The parties aren't happening only in the computer labs. During the last several years, the demand for instant Internet availability has spread so rapidly that many colleges with crowded computer labs now ship hundreds of additional terminals and modems into newly created computer residence halls. These designated lounges are stationed right inside the dormitories, so students need no longer even walk across campus to plug into their favorite chat room. Some colleges even provide a modem and free Internet access in students' individual rooms. Most computer residence halls have replaced TV lounges or other open meeting spaces, but few students protest. As we near the dawn of a new century, TV is out. The Net is in.

"Staying up late at night on the Internet is the best time I have at school," reveals Kim, a sophomore physics major and regular attendee of the kind of party we just witnessed. "After awhile, it was all I wanted to do, all I thought about. It was all so fascinating. In the chat rooms, I met a woman from Ottawa, Canada, who was a physics major at a university there. I don't see many women physics majors where I am. And I became close friends with a guy living in England, who was actually an exchange student from California. We connected over everything in life!"

Kim got so engrossed in her Net world that she ignored her studies. A former math and science whiz in high school with serious career ambitions, she allowed her grades to crash before recognizing that her new obsession was sabotaging her goals. When we met Kim briefly in our discussion of the Terminal Time Warp in Chapter 2, she just had tried and failed to quit the Internet cold turkey before understanding the power of this addiction. Now she's seeking help through a campus counselor and the kinds of recovery strategies we've outlined so far.

At least Kim recognized the problem. Most netheads, sadly, do not. And as their numbers continue to soar, colleges may be becoming the major breeding ground of Internet addiction. For example, when the dropout rate at Alfred University in Alfred, New York, more than doubled recently, Provost W. Richard Ott wanted to find out why. He couldn't see any logical explanation for why so many students who had arrived in college with SAT scores of 1,200 or higher would fail so quickly. An in-house survey revealed that 43 percent of these dropouts had been staying up late at night logged on to the Internet. "It's ironic," Ott said, "we've put all this money in for an educational tool, and some students are using it for self-destruction." Connie Beckman, director of Alfred's computing services, said "through educational programs designed to increase awareness of the danger of Net abuse, heavy pattern use dropped to 19 percent in this year's freshman class."

Here's a quick look at the contributing factors to such rampant Internet overuse:

■ *Free and unlimited Internet access.* When freshmen register today, they get a student ID card, a meal card, and most important, a free personal e-mail account. They've got no on-line service fees to pay, no limits to their time logged on, and computer labs open for their convenience round-the-clock. It's an Internet user's dream.

■ *Huge blocks of unstructured time.* Most college students attend classes for 12 to 16 hours per week. The rest of the time is their own to read, study, go to movies or parties, join clubs, or explore the new environment outside their campus walls. Many forget all those other activities and concentrate on one thing: the Internet.

■ *Newly experienced freedom from parental control.* Away from home and their parent's watchful eyes, college students long have exercised their new freedom by engaging in pranks, talking to friends to all hours of the night, sleeping with their boyfriends and girlfriends, and eating and drinking things Mom and Dad would not approve of. Today, they utilize that freedom by hanging out in the MUDs and chat rooms of cyberspace, and no parent can complain about on-line service fees or their refusal to eat dinner with the family or help out with chores.

■ *No monitoring or censoring of what they say or do on-line.* When they move on to the job world, college students may find suspicious bosses peeking over their shoulder or even monitoring their on-line time and usage. Even e-mail to coworkers could be intercepted by the wrong party. In college, no one's watching. Computer lab monitors tend to be student volunteers whose only responsibility is to assist anyone who needs help understanding how to use the Internet, not tell them what they can or cannot do on it.

- *Full encouragement from faculty and administrators.* Students understand that their school's administration and faculty want them to make full use of the Internet's vast resources. Abstaining from all Net use is seldom an option; in some large classes, professors place required course materials solely on the Net and engage in their only one-on-one contact with students through e-mail! Administrators, of course, want to see their major investments in computers and Internet access justified.

- *Adolescent training in similar activities.* By the time most kids get to college, they will have spent years staring at video game terminals, closing off the world around them with Walkmans, and engaging in that rapid-fire clicking of the TV remote. Even if they didn't get introduced to the Internet in high school, those other activities have made students well suited to slide into aimless Web surfing, skill-testing MUDs, and rat-a-tat-tat chat-room dialogue.

- *The desire to escape college stressors.* Students feel the pressures of making top grades, fulfilling parental expectations, and, upon graduation, facing fierce competition for good jobs. The Internet, ideally, would help make it easier for them to do their necessary course work as quickly and efficiently as possible. Instead, many students turn to their Net friends to hide from their difficult feelings of fear, anxiety, and depression.

- *Social intimidation and alienation.* With as many as 30,000 students on some campuses, students can easily get lost in the crowd. When they try to reach out, they often run into even tighter clicks than the in crowds of high school. Maybe they don't dress right or look right. But when they join the faceless community of the Internet, they find that with little effort they can become popular with new "friends" throughout the United States and in England, Australia, Germany, France, Hungary, Japan, New Zealand, and China. Why bother trying to socialize on campus?

■ *A higher legal drinking age.* With the drinking age at 21 in most states, undergraduate students can't openly drink alcohol and socialize in bars. So the Internet becomes a substitute drug of choice for many: no ID required and no closing hour!

With so many signs on campus pointing toward heavy reliance on the Internet, it's little wonder that when respondents to my Internet addiction survey were asked to name their main complications from excess on-line usage, academic problems ranked No. 1. When I asked respondents to identify which problem areas they would rate severe, 58 percent mentioned academic woes. Fifty-three percent referred to relationship issues, 52 percent cited Internet-related financial burdens, and 51 percent said their jobs were impacted. Internet addiction, clearly, has hit college students especially hard.

## First Year Away from Home

Amy is a freshman at a small liberal arts college in Illinois. Before going away to college, her only computer experience consisted of typing a few high school papers on her parents' PC. A few weeks into her first semester, she ventured into her college's computer lab, seeking only to learn how to send e-mail to her friends back home to ease her loneliness. Then her roommate introduced her to a popular Web chat room, and Amy tapped into a wide social circle of teens, college students, and adults from

Buffalo to Brussels. Soon she fell into a 54-hour-a-week Internet habit and a growing attachment to her California net brother Jim, whom she missed desperately when she went home for Thanksgiving.

"I tried to hide how depressed I was that weekend, but everyone could see it," Amy explains. "I tried writing snail-mail letters to Jim and my other Net friends, but it just wasn't the same. Even when I went out with my old friends from home, I was thinking about my new friends and couldn't wait until I got back to school, I guess it was like withdrawal."

Back on campus, Amy plunged into her Internet world with renewed vigor. She even made a few acquaintances at her college—fellow netheads, of course. Every day they met together for lunch and dinner and gossiped about what was going on in their favorite chat rooms. These five coeds gave themselves nicknames stemming from Internet terms: Gopher for Amy, and Usenet, Archie, Veronica, and Webster for the others. They called themselves the Net Family. They marched off to the computer lab as a group right after dinner and left together at 3 or 4 A.M. They joked about being addicted, but within the security and acceptance of this college "click," they believed their actions were natural—until first semester grades came in. Amy got a 1.2, not exactly what her parents expected from their former straight-A high school student.

"They thought I was spending too much time at real frat parties," Amy admits. "I was too embarrassed to tell them that I never went to class in the morning because I was too tired from chatting on the Internet most of the night, and that I never studied because I'd rather spend my time on-line."

Now frightened by her behavior and its consequences, Amy knew she had to do something. Like Kim, she tried to quit cold turkey. She didn't even go near the computer lab, doing homework assignments on her roommate's computer with no modem or Internet access. For three weeks, she daydreamed and fidgeted during class and when she tried to read her course books, she'd see imaginary chat-room dialogue scroll down the pages. Now that her fellow Internet users on campus found they had little in common with Amy, she lost her Net Family. When she tried to reach out to others, she discovered that they already had formed their primary friendships during those first weeks when she was holed up in the computer labs. Feeling more alone than ever, she rushed back home to the Net.

"I couldn't find Jim and a few of my other friends online, but many of the regulars were still there," she said. "I also made some new connections. I met Hans, and we started dating. He was just amazing!"

Hans lives in Germany. Their dating consisted mostly of shared chat-room dialogue and e-mail messages, though they did progress to swapping photos and a few actual cards and letters. But they never met in person, never even talked on the phone because neither could afford the long-distance charges. Both were thankful that their respective universities had supplied them with one means to a cross-continent courtship, free of charge.

## A MEGA MARRIAGE

Brian, a sophomore engineering major at the University of Oklahoma, took his on-line loving a step further—he "married" her. Coming from a small town, Brian lacked the confidence to join any college clubs in his first few weeks at school, and he was too shy to approach girls on campus. But when he became a champion MUDder, his popularity soared. For one solid week, he remained logged on to the game Mega Wars 24 hours straight, pausing only for an occasional break or a nap with the computer still tuned in to the action. In his character of Lazarus, Brian rose to the level of Admiral of the Empire. His men trusted and respected him, rival troops from the Coalition feared him, and women of his empire adored him. He selected the lovely Heron to be his wife, and their wedding was announced within the text of the game:

> *Hear ye, hear ye. Gather at the castle at 10 pm tomorrow. Lazarus and Heron are to be wed! All are invited to offer praise and devotion to the Admiral and his bride.*

At the appointed hour, more than 60 regulars of the game arrived at the castle for this Mega wedding. The "minister" stood before the assembled to officiate the ceremony. Heron was resplendent in white gown with pearls and sequins. Lazarus was dressed in full uniform. When these "virtual" vows were pronounced, attendees raised their wine goblets in a toast: "Long live Lazarus! Long live Heron!"

As the game continues in the days and weeks ahead, their marriage will be recognized by all players. Brian has a mate for life—his MUD life anyway. In real life, Brian teeters on the edge of flunking out of college. Unlike Amy, he lacks even the presence of a Net Family of campus pals because he's got Internet access on his own computer in his dorm room. He's also using the privacy to indulge in smoking marijuana. Stoned on pot, his lines between virtual reality and life are becoming increasingly blurred. Parading around as an admiral with wife in tow may seem all too real to him, until he finds himself booted out of college and back in his hometown with no degree, no job, no real friends—and no wife.

# THE DISTORTED VIEW
# FROM THE IVORY TOWER

Alfred University's positive response to Net abuse, re-
counted on page 176, is unfortunately atypical among
college administrators and faculty so far. As rampant as
Internet addiction may be on campus, most academicians who peek in on their packed computer labs can see
nothing but dedicated students and the benefits of new
technology. They don't see students spending up to 60 or
more hours per week using that new technology to avoid
their studies while addictive patterns threaten their academic and psychological well-being. They honestly believe that students sitting at their terminals must be working diligently on research papers, when if they zoomed in
on the computer screens of average collegiate Internet
users they'd see a completely different picture:

■ Chat-room dialogue about the frustrations of irrele-
vant college courses and those demanding and out-
of-touch parents back home, as well as plenty of on-line
romancing. College Internet users indeed may be challenging themselves to learn and stretch beyond previous
limits, but rather than sticking to any course syllabus
they're more apt to be undertaking the kind of study one
of my survey respondents shared with me. As a feminist,
she traveled the meeting rooms in the persona of a sexist
man to see how it felt from the other side.

■ Dedication and devotion toward MUD games that
never end, challenging the college player to stay logged
on for 10 to 20 hours every day to perfect his or her skills
and rise to the level of Lazarus. When you glance at a serious MUDder in action, you would swear that person is
engaged in the most intense and difficult studying of any
student. But you won't find much calculus in Mega Wars.

■ Downloading pornographic photos and other forms of cyberporn. While cybersex may be a bit too personal for crowded computer labs, many college students still check out the sexier chat, even if only to poke fun at what they regard as silly adults.

■ Exchanging e-mail with their real-life friends back home or at other colleges, or sending e-mail to their new nethead companions in far-off locales. From my survey, I would say that some students channel most of their creative energy into writing these messages. Unfortunately, as many students themselves admit and my colleagues in the teaching ranks frequently lament, students get so used to the shorthand, stream-of-consciousness style of writing that dominates e-mail and chat rooms that they lose all ability to write proper, understandable English on school papers.

■ Scanning newsgroup postings to stay abreast of the latest info about their favorite movies, TV shows, musical groups, UFO sightings, the weather, juicy rumors about politicians, or their favorite forms of trivia. Students who spend large chunks of their time tuning into these newsgroups find whatever's on their selected newsgroups infinitely more intriguing than researching history papers.

■ Endless surfing of Web pages on any and all topics that catch their eye. While Web-browsing students at least may be exposing themselves to other cultures, it's often through a primitive Web page constructed by a 14-year-old. Even a more industrious student who may start out searching the Web on a sincere class-related mission easily can fall into the Terminal Time Warp, spending three or four hours meandering side streets to nowhere.

But without the zoom lens to focus on what's really on students' computer terminals, it's understandable that college presidents and deans of student affairs hail the late-night action in the computer labs as a positive sign. After all, students who frequent the labs aren't drinking or taking drugs. They're not watching TV or hanging out in video arcades. They're not driving around the surrounding city or town with radio blaring until 3 A.M. triggering complaints from local police. They're not spending all their time sunning themselves on the campus grounds or tossing frisbees at the stadium. They are utilizing the technology that keeps old State U. on the cutting edge of progress. And rather than brooding alone in their dorm rooms, they apparently are keeping busy.

Faculty are no more likely than administrators to sniff out the signs of Internet addiction under their noses. Students may cut morning classes, fail to study, turn in lackluster papers, and sit silent and stone-faced despite the instructors' best efforts at inspiring lively class discussions. But faculty often shrug off such behavior as indicative of our times, with students generally more apathetic, distant, and limited by attention spans shortened from years of being glued to the TV.

Then again, even those faculty who do recognize that students waste huge blocks of potential study time playing around on the Internet usually deny that any real problem could come from that. Why? They're probably hooked on the Net themselves! Like students, faculty enjoy free and unlimited Internet access and a good bit of unstructured time, along with the added temptation of a private office so no one can see what they're "working on" behind closed doors.

I've talked to many faculty who admitted frittering away several hours between classes and appointments browsing the Web, scanning newsgroups, and even chatting and MUDding. One computer science instructor confessed that when he lost access to his favorite MUD game, he flipped out—then shared his frustration with his understanding students in class. Like any other segment of the adult population, college teachers are subject to the same kind of psychological and emotional struggles that can trigger addictive behavior.

What about college counseling centers? Do counselors understand the signs of Internet addiction, its prevalence in their communities, and how to assist a student hooked on the Net? A few have begun to respond to this new obsession and its impact on students.

Jonathan Kandell, assistant director of the counseling center at the University of Maryland, launched an Internet addiction support group on his campus. Kathleen Scherer, a staff psychologist who uncovered evidence of this obsession through her own survey at the University of Texas, presented a campuswide seminar titled, "It's 4 A.M., and I Can't—Uh—Won't Log Off." Only a handful of students responded to her initial overtures to talk about their problems in public, but others did seek out Dr. Scherer for help with their Internet obsession in private. And when any student comes to the counseling center with presenting problems of depression or poor grades, she has the knowledge and awareness to ask about Internet usage.

At most universities, however, counselors know little or nothing about the ways of the Internet and its special allure for students. One college counselor aware of my study called to explain a typical experience. She was treating a female student who reported feeling extremely depressed because of a recent breakup with her boyfriend. The counselor assumed the boy was another student at that college or a former beau from back home. Not until their fifth session, and only by accident, did the counselor learn that this "boyfriend" existed only in cyberspace. Yet the girl's devastation appeared just as real as if she had known him in real life. The counselor asked me whether such things were prevalent on the Internet and how a young adult could get so emotionally attached to a computer pal.

## BREAKING DOWN THE CAMPUS WALLS OF DENIAL

When I lecture about Internet addiction on college campuses today, the college people who seek me out most often are computer science professors who have had a close-up view of on-line obsession for several years. Many of their classes, in fact, are conducted almost entirely through the computer. "We know this abusive behavior on the Internet has been going on for a long time," they tell me. "Kids start out doing all the relevant course work on the computer, then they get sidetracked by all the other stuff and you can't get them focused on their work. They really do get hooked and we're glad that a professional psychologist recognizes this and is trying to do something about it."

But the most enthusiastic response to my lectures comes from students themselves. After I outline the signs of Internet addiction and describe some of the case studies from colleges like theirs, often as many as half the students in the audience rush to tell me the profile fits perfectly—for someone they know. As is true with adult cyberwidows, Internet addiction college-style is detected more easily by students whose friend or lover has gotten lost in cyberspace. From their vantage point close to the behavior, these students readily spot the signs of trouble in the nethead in their life.

- Lack of sleep and excess fatigue.
- Declining grades.
- Less investment in relationships with boyfriend or girlfriend.

- Withdrawal from all campus social activities and events.
- General apathy, edginess, or irritability when off-line (cybershakes).
- Denial of the seriousness of the problem.
- Rationalizing that what they learn on the Net is superior to their classes.
- Lying about how much time they spend on-line and what they do there.
- Trying to quit completely when threatened with possible expulsion because of poor grades, then slipping right back into the same addictive patterns.

Denial cuts especially deep in the college environment because packed computer labs provide an even more effective cover than drinking in a crowded bar. When you're sitting in rows of Internet users whose obsessions manifest in eight-hour sessions, no one's going to tap you on the shoulder and say: "Hey, I think you're seriously addicted to what you do on the computer and you need to get some help." Like Amy in her protected Net Family, most netheads laugh off any suggestion that they're becoming psychologically dependent on the feelings they get from MUDs and chat rooms. "Only foolish adults get addicted to stuff they take or things they do," students counter. "Anyway, I'm not as bad as the geeks with the computer majors who never log off and have to know all the software programs. I can cut back or quit fooling around on the Net any time I want."

Then serious trouble sets in: They flunk out of college. Their real-life girlfriend or boyfriend breaks up with them because all they ever want to do is play on the Net. Their parents explode when they find out their huge investment in their child's college education is going to support all-night nethead parties. They fall into a major depression when their on-line steady blips off the screen forever. They experience major withdrawal when they try to quit their habit, even if their only motivation was to stay in school to keep their free Internet access. At that point, the addicted students themselves at last may decide to seek help.

### *Assisting the College Internet Addict*

If you're a college nethead yourself or a counselor seeing students who exhibit the warning signs of Internet addiction, here are five helpful tips for recovery:

1. *Educate yourself about the problem.* If you're a counselor, learn all you can about the Internet and what students do there. Talk to students about their on-line activities, ask them questions about what they get out of it, go on-line yourself to see what chat rooms and MUDs look like in action. During intake interviews with students reporting depression or anxiety, make sure you inquire about their Internet habits.

If you're a student, learn all you can about how behavioral addictions function. Eating disorders and gambling addictions lead to many of the same symptoms as Internet addiction, and if you go to a counselor who's initially skeptical when you say you're hooked on the Net, explain the similarities with these recognized addictions. Remember that it's unwise to quit cold turkey on your own. As Amy learned, withdrawal is painful; you may be able to alleviate the major problems you're experiencing through some adjustments of your usage.

2. *Eliminate your most destructive Internet habits.* Where do you or the student you know spend most of the Internet time: chat rooms, MUDs, cyberporn, newsgroups, the Web? You may need to eliminate that one application

while using the Net on a limited basis for e-mail or legitimate research for classes. For Brian, that means no more MUDding; for Amy, it's curtains on the chat rooms. Time-management techniques, unfortunately, are less likely to work for students than for adults with personal computers at home because of the campus peer pressure. Limiting yourself to one hour on a MUD in the midst of a hopping computer lab is like an alcoholic trying to stay sober in a bar or someone with an eating disorder lingering around a bakery.

Once you've regained control of your Internet habit and get your grades back on track, you may return to the computer labs and try short, tightly scheduled sessions on your favorite Internet applications. But for now, stay out of the danger zone as much as possible. Type your papers on your own computer or one without a modem, while redirecting your energy elsewhere.

3. *Enter the social world your campus offers.* If you look a little harder, you may find that the unique college environment really can offer many of the same social benefits of the Internet—or more. Find a club or organization that matches your preaddiction interests or a new area you discovered on-line. If you enjoyed creating witty e-mail messages or chat-room notes in cyberspace, write a column for the college newspaper or put up a bulletin board notice announcing your interest in forming a writers' circle or poets' society. Go to all your classes and talk to classmates afterward. Attend school events. If many of your Net friends attend some other college, chances are that in your own college of 1,000 or 20,000 students you can find someone or some group you can relate to as easily as you connected with your cyberfriends.

4. *Discover your campus library.* I'm amazed when I talk to students who tell me they never set foot inside the library

(unless the computer lab is there). They say they can find anything they want on the Net while saving time because they don't have to get up from their seats. They're fooling themselves. Though the information superhighway can be a valuable research aide, the library offers a stronger organization that still may guide you to the desired material more efficiently. You'll also find real books to open and sink your teeth into, something the average Web page simply can't match. While you're discovering the world of books in the library, you may notice that it's a quiet place quite conducive to studying, something you can't say about sitting amid rows of computer terminals. So find a comfortable spot, take out your course books and catch up with what you've been neglecting.

5. *Teach your fellow students about Internet addiction.* College is a learning environment, and students often can be the best teachers. If you've had problems stemming from your obsession with the Internet, you can provide a great service to others in your school by urging them to consider the harmful effects of abusing their on-line privileges and free time. Talk to your old nethead friends. Show them this book. If they appear too intimidated to speak to their concerns in front of their Net Family, invite them to see you privately and ask you questions about your experiences, or steer them toward a counselor. Bring up the subject at an appropriate moment in a class discussion. Or, for greater immediate impact, you may choose to go on-line with your story in hopes of encouraging other college students to seriously examine their own behavior.

## A Learned Response
## from the Academic Community

Over the last few years, as news of my study has spread, I have received many e-mail messages and phone calls from students eager to conduct their own research into the dynamics of on-line obsessions. Undergraduate and graduate students in both psychology and sociology were eager to survey their own campuses or go on-line directly in search of signs of Internet addiction and to test its causes, its similarity to other addictions, and the implications for university populations. Many of these student researchers admitted that they themselves had been using the Net excessively but had recognized the problem and made adjustments in their behavior. Their new endeavors, along with the first few counseling support groups and seminars for college Internet addicts, signal hope that colleges can take the lead in expanding awareness of this societal problem and creating solutions for it.

But it will be a long road from general denial to the implementation of specific change, and students need help today. That means counselors must become better educated about the problem and invite an open dialogue about the Internet—how we all use it and how it may be impacting us. Faculty need to be more clear with students regarding just when Internet use is expected of them and needed for class assignments, and when they'd still recommend traditional research tools such as the library and field explorations. Faculty sit in the best position to warn students not to get so swept away by the dazzling allure of cyberspace that they forget to read their books for class or study other course material.

College administrators may need to put their foot down on that unlimited Internet access. At Ohio State University, students now are restricted to six hours per day on the Internet because of the limited number of modems and the large number of students who stay on the Net for long stretches of time. Similar rules should be considered by other colleges large and small regarding total number of log-ins or a maximum number of hours per week.

Also, college officials should consider banning access to chat rooms and MUDs from all terminals in computer labs. At the labs, signs should be posted urging students not to abuse their Internet privileges and reminding them that the computers are for school use only, not entertainment. Computer lab monitors should be encouraged to watch more closely for students who spend hours fiddling with the social aspects of the Net and to advise the director of computer services. When trends are detected, an appropriate campuswide intervention could be arranged.

No official at any university would ever promote opening an all-night bar on campus. Yet what college decision makers need to realize today is that by granting students unlimited Internet access at 24-hour computer labs, they've opened the door to addictive behavior with many of the same harmful consequences. The sad truth is that while netheads have been staying up almost all night with worsening on-line obsessions, faculty and administrators have been asleep to the problem. It's about time they woke up.

## EIGHT

# No Work Today—Everybody's Gone Surfin'

*If he only knew that my addiction was to the Internet, and that he was supplying the dope!*—RON, A PRODUCT MANAGER, SPEAKING OF HIS EMPLOYER

"I needed help, but they treated me like a criminal," the distressed woman on the phone tells me. "I'm a sane person: I just felt compelled to keep using the Internet the way I did."

Evelyn had just been fired from her job as an executive secretary at an aerospace engineering firm in northern California. Less than a month earlier she had been promoted by the same company after only a year and a half on the job, a clear sign of how much they valued her work and trusted in her continued ability to serve them. Instead, just as she settled into her new job, she was informed that she was being suspended for time card fraud. She hadn't been legitimately at work for much of the time on her card, they contended, because for many of those work hours she actually was engaged in Internet activity for personal use.

The morning Evelyn returned from her suspension, her employer and the company's human resources manager were waiting for her. As she sat down, they dumped a thick pile of computer printouts in front of her. The printouts displayed actual logs of all her Internet activity

194

in the two weeks before her suspension: an accounting of every e-mail sent and received and her total time spent in the Inter-Relay Chat system. Through these records, they had computed that more than 50 percent of her alleged work time had been eaten up by unauthorized use of the Net. She was dismissed from her job immediately.

Evelyn had become a victim of another major complication of Internet addiction. Fifty-one percent of the respondents in my study reported severe job-related problems due to their excessive on-line usage. More and more workers are gaining Internet privileges on the job, and many find themselves getting hooked almost overnight on Net features completely unrelated to their work tasks. Employees find it simple to make vacation plans or shop for a new car on-line. Employers are beginning to catch on.

One survey of 150 executives from the nation's top 1,000 companies revealed that 55 percent of all managers believe that time surfing the Internet for nonbusiness purposes is undermining their employees' effectiveness on the job. New monitoring devices allow employers to track Internet usage, and initial results confirm their worst suspicions. One major company tracked all traffic going across its Internet connection and discovered that only 23 percent of the usage was business-related!

There is a growing availability of such monitoring software as employers not only fear poor productivity but find they need to stop the use of valuable network resources for nonbusiness purposes. The potential for legal liability also exists: An employee may violate software licensing laws by illegally downloading unlicensed software or conduct personal business from the company server. But "Big Brother" is watching as this software provides managers with detailed reports of information like the most popular Web sites, the most active users, and Internet usage logged by time of day. And it's all completely nonobtrusive so that employees will never know who is snooping.

However, the president of a Long Island engineering firm said, "We had one major incident of abuse, and considered this software, but it was too expensive." Depending on the types of functions and the number of users the software needs to monitor, the cost can be as much as $15,000 to install. Managers struggle to justify the costs for the reported benefits. And new questions arise: Will we need to purchase additional network equipment to make this software compatible? Do we have to monitor every employee? Who will have access to the network traffic reports?

When a manager learns workers have gone surfin' half the day, the workers get reprimanded. If employees are fortunate, that reprimand comes first in the form of a warning or suspension. But because these once dependable employees don't understand the nature of the addictive pull that's sucked them into this worker wasteland, they may feel powerless to stop. At some point, the employer gets intolerant of the loss of work productivity and terminates the employee. Along the way, both parties suffer a rapid erosion of trust.

"It's not fair to fire me for using the Internet when you tell me I need to use it for my job," the worker argues. "And it's certainly not right for you to be spying on my private interactions on-line. What I say or do under my log-in should be my business. Anyway, I couldn't have been abusing it nearly as much as you say I did."

"We need the Internet to streamline communication, increase productivity, research potential new trends, target a growing on-line market, and keep up with our competitors," the employer counters. "But you workers keep spending all your time posting personal e-mail to friends and playing those silly games and talking in chat groups. If we don't get rid of you when we catch you, we'd never get any work done here."

Both parties agree on one point. Once the problem surfaces, it doesn't take long to boil over into serious trouble. Let's take a closer look at Evelyn's story to learn how and why.

## SOMEONE MAY BE WATCHING YOU

"It all happened so fast I hardly even had a chance to understand it," explains Evelyn, who at age 47 feels especially insecure about her future employment prospects. "I didn't even know what the Internet was until a few months ago. That's when we all went on-line at work."

Evelyn remembers that first day in early February clearly. Her close friend Diana, whom she recently had told of this new development on her job, sent her flowers—virtual flowers that appeared only on the computer screen—to welcome her to the world of the Internet. Diana also initiated Evelyn into the chat rooms to show her just how friendly everyone was there and the special things the regulars would do or say for one another. The following week, Evelyn devoted her lunch break to sending special Valentine's Day messages to the chat group. "I knew that many of them were homebound, single, and lonely," she recalls. "I wanted to cheer them up."

When Evelyn got home she shared her excitement about this new work device with Eric, her husband of 19 years. He agreed that it sounded like fun and got a modem and on-line service for their home. Right away, they journeyed into an over-40 chat room. With Evelyn sitting at the terminal and Eric watching over her shoulder, a user with the handle "Lonely Married Man" invited her to a private room to chat alone. Within minutes, he was urging her to join him in describing their mutual erotic fantasies, even as she typed: "My husband's here with me." The response came back: "Okay with me if okay with you two." Evelyn grinned sheepishly, and as Eric nodded self-consciously she flung herself fully into her first cybersex encounter. That night, she and Eric enjoyed their most passionate lovemaking in years.

Evelyn assumed this encounter would be a onetime thing, but the next morning she was greeted by an e-mail message from Lonely Married Man telling her that he really wanted to chat with her again soon, this time out of eyesight of her husband. Though she would never agree to such an invitation from a real person, she decided it wouldn't do any harm just to talk to him through e-mail. So at work that day she answered him back, and they began an ongoing, nonsexual discussion about their work, their marriages, and anything else that popped up. He was only 31, and Evelyn enjoyed this apparently harmless means of having a younger man as a special friend.

In the same chat room she also met Prince of Tides, the on-line handle of a 55-year-old Florida businessman. Their conversation was generally innocent with only a bit of flirting, but Evelyn joked to herself that now she had a younger man and an older man pursuing her.

Eric, however, noticed that Evelyn hardly mentioned the chat rooms after that one cybersex encounter he witnessed in their study at home. He decided to check up on her. Using her on-line handle "Monica," he caught on to her male admirers in cyberspace and asked her to stop immediately. Evelyn understood his jealousy and notified her two cyberbeaus that they needed to cool it to keep peace at home. Neither man took the brush-off lightly. Lonely Married Man typed: "Don't forget me, Monica. I love you!" Prince of Tides sent her virtual flowers with the note: "Please reconsider." And she did.

"I felt like I just couldn't stop carrying on these on-line friendships," she explains. "I wasn't really unhappy in my marriage, but after 20 years with the same husband, it felt so refreshing to be valued and wanted by these two other guys. I felt so much younger. And they seemed to need whatever they got from me in our talks. I didn't want to let them down."

So Evelyn ran back to her cyberbeaus. Up to this point, she had limited her chatting well enough to keep up with her work flow and even earn that promotion. Her workstation had been in a private corner, as well, so no one was likely to spot anything on her computer screen that would arouse suspicion. But her promotion meant moving to a more visible workstation, while her addiction to the Internet intensified. She even went hunting for new men to banter with, and as she spent more than half her workday typing notes to them, a coworker noticed what she was up to and reported her to management. The systems manager in charge of the company's computer operations was assigned to monitor Evelyn's Internet time and use, and soon she was "busted."

Even before Evelyn was suspended, she did seek help. She visited her company's Employee Assistance Program (EAP) representative and explained what she had been doing on the Internet and how she couldn't stop. "Sounds like you have marital problems—go get couples counseling," she was advised. Her actual obsession with the Internet chat rooms and her dependency on the good feelings she got in flirting with men were never seriously addressed.

Unfortunately, this is the norm in most workplaces today. If previously valued workers are detected with a drinking problem that begins to interfere with their work performance, EAP personnel may well refer them to a recovery program at a rehab clinic—paid at the company's expense—with their jobs waiting for them when they get out. But when Internet addicts knock on the same EAP door for assistance, they find no helping hand. Instead, they are left to deal with the knee-jerk reaction of management who treat them, as Evelyn described, like criminals.

# WHEN YOUR BOSS SUPPLIES THE DRUG

Sometimes an employer does suspect that addiction may be the root cause of poor job performance, but when the Internet is involved, employers don't yet know the right questions. So they go hunting in the wrong direction. We can see this in the case of Ron, a product manager for a Pittsburgh manufacturing firm who until recently had excelled in his work. But in the last two months, he missed a few important deadlines and his overall productivity had dipped dramatically. Yet in the same period Ron was working extra hours, coming in unscheduled most Saturdays and arriving two hours early every morning. It didn't add up. So when Ron sat down for his annual job review, his boss searched for an answer.

"First he asked me if I was having family problems and I said no," Ron recalls. "He asked me if I was using alcohol or drugs and I said no. Had I gotten into trouble by gambling too much? No. If he only knew that my addiction was to the Internet, and that he was supplying the dope!"

But his boss never asked, and Ron never volunteered the truth about what he now began to recognize as a problem. Two months earlier he had been given an Internet account to help streamline his ordering and research new contacts. He made plenty of "contacts" all right, but not the kind his boss had in mind.

Only 26, Ron was strongly motivated to rise through the company ranks, so he figured the more he mastered this new tool, the better his chances for promotion. He stopped going out to lunch with his buddies, choosing to stay behind to learn how to navigate the Net. One day, after sending and receiving dozens of e-mail messages during his lunch hour, he browsed some Web sites. Next time he looked up to check the time, his lunch hour had been up for two hours! He quickly resumed his usual work tasks.

Back on the Net during lunch hour the next day, Ron stumbled upon *alt.sex.stories,* where Internet users share real and fictitious accounts of their sexual adventures. Still single, Ron enjoyed renting an occasional X-rated video at home and even had tried a 900 number phone sex service once, so he found the kinky dialogue titillating. Then he went on to the huge assortment of cyberporn and the sexually explicit chat areas. Now he was staying logged on until late afternoon and was getting behind in his work. No problem, he figured. He'd just come in Saturday and catch up.

"But when I came in Saturday, there was that damned machine just sitting there tempting me," he admits. "Plus, it was much quieter in the office, so I had more privacy. I stayed on the Net all day."

Now Ron was keeping up with some of the women he met via frequent e-mail, and he even had joined some newsgroups. Without a home computer, he was doing all his surfing at work and his habit quickly soared to more than 25 hours per week, all ostensibly while on the job. After receiving his poor evaluation at that job review, Ron just had begun to try to cut down when his boss decided to monitor his Internet activity. When confronted with the hard evidence of Ron's cyberporn-peeping and other sexual shenanigans, his boss fired him on the spot. Like Evelyn, Ron had suffered the harshest possible penalty for losing control of a habit triggered only when his employer supplied the drug.

## ADDICTED AT HOME, USELESS AT WORK

You don't need an on-line hookup on your job for your work performance to be affected by Internet addiction. In fact, you don't even have to work in an environment where computers are involved to stumble into Net trouble. Toby, like many survey respondents I interviewed, found that getting hooked at home undermined his job effectiveness. An auto mechanic in the Philadelphia area, Toby had bought a home computer for his family a few months before he contacted me. He intended to teach his two kids how to use it for school, but after he went MUD-ding a few times the computer became his personal toy.

"I named my character Vader after the Star Wars character Darth Vader. I just couldn't believe how much fun it was, and how quickly time flew by," Toby explains. "Pretty soon I was staying up until 2 or 3 in the morning every night, and that's not a good move when you have to be at work by 7."

Arriving at work exhausted, he began messing up: forgetting to put in a parts order one day, failing to tighten a hose the next. A few times he caught himself sleeping on his back under a car. Already a heavy coffee drinker, he resorted to the heftier boost from caffeine pills in a frantic attempt to stay alert. He also could see his moods changing drastically. Always considered easygoing and ready to tell or listen to a good joke, Toby now turned away from his coworkers when they approached him with a juicy story. More than once, he snapped at a good friend. Toby had a good idea what was causing this change, but he wasn't about to tell the guys.

"None of them even used computers, and they had no clue what the Internet was," he relates. "Even if I tried to explain it to them, they'd think I was crazy and just laugh it all off. I'd become the big joke of the shop."

Toby did his best to regulate his usage. He figured that if he cut out the late-night MUDding and only played in the morning before work, he'd get enough sleep to work efficiently and still get his kicks from the game. So he tried going to bed at 10 and getting up at 5, but 90 minutes wasn't nearly enough time for a good MUD session. He played right on past 7 and began arriving late for work. Then he left early a few times because he just had to go home to get some sleep, and he even called in sick on several occasions because he had gained some MUDding proficiency and wanted to stay on an entire day to see how high he could rise.

Toby's boss didn't know what had caused this declining work performance and changed behavior. But he did know that the head mechanic position for which Toby had been the leading candidate now would go to someone else. He called Toby in for a meeting and gave him a warning: Either get back to his former solid work habits or lose his job.

"That was a real wake-up call for me," recalls Toby, who saw an article about my survey a week later and called me seeking help. "I felt really stupid that this was happening to me, but I couldn't deny that the Internet was messing up my work life."

I suggested that Toby set up a strict, limited schedule of his MUDding sessions in early evening, and to help him through his choice points I advised that he fill out and carry reminder cards listing the five harmful effects of using the Net and the five benefits of moderated usage. I also urged him to find some noncomputer games to play with his kids, where he could access the same imaginative powers he had tapped into in his Vader role. Toby at least had another chance, in part because his boss had no actual evidence of what had begun to encroach on his work time and efficiency. Had he been using the Net on the job, he might have been booted out as quickly as Ron and Evelyn.

As a worker fired for Internet abuse struggles to adjust to unemployment, the resulting depression and anxiety over financial burdens often worsen the addiction. Not long after I had heard from Toby, Walter contacted me to share his experiences after losing his job as a shipping clerk because of spending too much work time on the

Net. Suddenly out of a job, Walter upped his Internet habit at home to more than 70 hours per week to escape his feelings of shame and fear. That led to higher on-line service fees and a higher pile of unpaid bills. In hopes of easing his debts, Walter asked his mother if he could borrow one of her credit cards. She refused.

"That just made me more desperate," Walter confesses. "One night I was over at her house, and while she sat in the living room I went to the kitchen to get a drink. I knew she always left her purse hanging over the kitchen chair. I carefully opened it up, got out her wallet, and took two of her credit cards. She still hasn't noticed they're missing."

## A NEED FOR RELIEF

Internet addiction is triggering serious work-related problems as rapidly as new features emerge in the information superhighway itself. Clearly, immediate help is needed. More companies in industries from engineering to journalism are venturing on-line every day. Others are expanding their numbers of employees with Internet access or giving them new on-line functions and assignments to handle. Along the way, employer distrust and suspicion regarding personal use of the Internet continue to rise.

But those employees busily exploring chat rooms, newsgroups, MUDs and rapid-fire e-mail exchanges usually are not sabotaging their work efforts intentionally. Sometimes they begin with a few minutes of simply checking the latest sports scores or stock market reports before realizing that three hours have slipped by. Often they're unaware of the suspicious spotlight cast toward their computer screens until it's too late. Neither party understands what's really happening nor recognizes that the problem could be addressed in a manner that keeps once-valued workers in the fold while rebuilding trust. By recognizing the workplace warning signs of Internet addiction and opening to the need for recovery strategies that fit this Internet-dependent community, employers and employees both will benefit.

## Learn the Workplace Warning Signs

The examples of Evelyn, Ron, and Toby illustrate many of the symptoms of Internet addiction on the job. Let's take a closer look at some of the main signs:

■ *Decrease in productivity.* Although many factors can contribute to a worker's diminished capacity to get the job done, companies that recently adopted the Internet should be especially sensitive to the possibility that output may be sagging because workers have discovered the Net's interactive applications that can hook anyone quickly. Workers likewise should know that if they're not as productive, those fun new games and chat rooms may be getting in the way.

■ *Increase in mistakes.* Most workers getting hooked on the Internet tend to shift back and forth rapidly between legitimate work and interactive Net play. This makes it more difficult to concentrate on work details, especially when they're spending a lot of time in MUDs or chat rooms, where little care is given to correct grammar, spelling, punctuation, or even logical thought patterns. Anything goes on the Internet, but not so with work details. An unaware worker may assume wrongly that her sudden increase in errors is being caused by anxiety about her work performance, when it's really triggered by bad habits cultivated on the Net.

- *Less interaction with coworkers.* As we've seen in our earlier explorations into addictive behavior, those who get caught in the Net frequently tune out all other social activity because of the relationships they're developing online. In the workplace, Internet addicts not only shun all coffee break chatter or friendly morning greetings, they also turn down invitations for shared lunches or after-hours socializing in favor of sticking with their chat-room regulars.

- *Startled looks when approached at their stations.* If the employee enjoys relative privacy during his or her computer usage, notice how he or she responds when approached unaware. Many workers flinch in their chairs, shift their bodies, or quickly type a command to change what's on their screens. If you're a worker experiencing such a response, take this as a cue that you're getting addicted and feeling a need to cover it up.

- *Less tolerant of workplace conditions.* A once agreeable employee may suddenly balk at requests to work overtime and in staff meetings mounts vehement protests about long-standing company policies and procedures. There could be a natural explanation—chat-room regulars in the workplace love to complain about their respective bosses and work conditions. The complaints may trigger action or at least a more sullen and withdrawn demeanor.

- *Excessive fatigue.* Internet addicts may be more tired on the job for several reasons. They know they're spending too much time goofing off on the Net, so like Ron they try to work extra hours to compensate and get exhausted by the effort. Or if the addiction is most prominent after work hours at home, the on-lineaholic is coming to work without much sleep, like Toby. Workers should recognize that if they're tired all the time at work, it may not be because their employer gave them more to do, but rather that they've given themselves more activities to keep up with in the form of personal Internet usage.

■ *More sick calls, tardiness, and midday doctor's appointments.* This warning sign relates more to workers who are using the Internet excessively at home, rather than at work. Like Toby, they're skipping out of work because they're so exhausted from surfing the Net late at night or they want to surf at home during the workday. These signs are frequently understood by bosses or human resource managers as indicators of a possible addiction. Now it's time to add Internet addiction to their list of possibilities.

It took decades for employers to recognize that it was in their best interest to invest in treatment programs for valued employees with drinking or drug problems. Employers would be making a major mistake if they endured several years of rampant Internet addiction and simply punished on-lineaholics in their workforce, rather than setting up the means to assist them. Excellent employees like Evelyn and Ron whose performances and behavior change almost overnight when they get hooked on the Net may be capable of successfully serving their companies for many years, if their problem is understood and treated with greater awareness and sensitivity.

Here and there, the need has been recognized. Sally Littell, consultant to the EAP program at The Gateway Rehabilitation Center in Aliquippa, Pennsylvania, reports that her agency has begun to see workers referred in the Pittsburgh area for their excessive Internet habits. "We shouldn't just dismiss workers for Internet misuse," says Littell. "We should instead try to understand the problem and treat it seriously. And we should encourage employees to seek help" (personal communication, June 16, 1997).

RECOVERY STRATEGY 17:

## Help for the Addicted Employee

While Internet addiction is not yet recognized officially as a clinical disorder that would enable a worker to receive insurance coverage for treatment, companies still can take four important steps to help their addicted employees:

1. *Ask the right questions.* If an employee displays many of the workplace warning signs of Internet addiction, managers or human resource specialists should ask direct questions about that person's use of the Internet. If it becomes clear that on-lineaholism has set in, rather than taking the hard-line approach of spying and punishment, make it clear that your intent is to work together to solve the problem if possible. Communicate your awareness that getting hooked on the Internet is a natural response to the temptation that comes from just getting an on-line account on the job or suddenly taking on more Net-related assignments. Make appropriate references to examples of other workers who became addicted to the Internet but found a way to manage their on-line usage. Treat the issue seriously by educating your workers, not threatening them.

2. *Determine whether your employee really wants help.* If your worker denies any problem with the Internet or simply declares he or she will cut out the abuse, give that person some information about Internet addiction to read or at least hold onto. You might recommend that your employee read this chapter and take the Internet Addiction Test in Chapter 1. Clarify your own expectations of the improvement you expect to see in that person's job performance and schedule a follow-up interview to assess how your worker is doing.

Let's say, however, that your employee does admit to wasting hours a day on personal e-mail, chat rooms, MUDs, or cyberporn and shares his or her embarrassment at losing control of the ability to stop or slow down. Workers may say they honestly regret what their abuse is costing the company. Perhaps they tell you they tried to curb the habit and that somehow it just didn't work. In this case, be prepared to refer them to where they can get help.

3. *Find a suitable recovery program or counselor.* Through your company's EAP or other outreach avenue, research your community for an addiction recovery treatment program that could integrate the specific issues of Internet addiction within their established programs for alcoholism or chemical dependency. However, don't insist that programs make abstinence from the Internet the goal. Rather, a program would be more effective if geared more toward the approach to eating disorders, stressing emotional awareness of the problem and teaching moderation techniques similar to those outlined in this book. After all, just as anyone with an eating disorder still must eat every day, any Internet addict with on-line job responsibilities still must log on regularly.

You also may find a respected individual therapist or counselor who recognizes Internet addiction as a legitimate problem and understands how to assist a client's recovery. Therapists may learn that they can diagnose the Internet addict as suffering from obsessive/compulsive disorder and thereby enable the worker to obtain insurance reimbursement for treatment. Employers must understand that they may initially have to take an active role in educating members of the therapeutic community about the dynamics of Internet addiction, how quickly it surfaces on the job, and what can be done to help the addicted worker. Employers have their fingers on the pulse of this problem, and they have the most to lose if it goes unchecked. It's in an employer's interest to help cultivate the resources to address the issue effectively.

4. *Tighten control of Internet access.* As employers establish outside resources to help employees who get hooked on the Net, they can actively assist in moderating Internet use with tighter controls in the work environment. Make an honest review of whether all your employees need full-time Net access. Many executives who rush to hook up their entire workforce to the Net simply don't understand the actual capability and limitations of this new device, and their computer systems managers often feel too intimidated to point out that the boss's idea of progress in this realm is a bit off-line. Why grant everyone unlimited Net access at their personal terminals when your company's need to use the Internet could be served with just one or a handful of on-line stations that employees would go to only when their work requires? To further discourage abusive use, put the Internet-access terminals in a public, visible location.

Or, if you believe that every employee needs to use the Internet for some regular work tasks, consider customizing access to match the requirements of individual workers. You could develop a system similar to a block of 900-line calls on employee telephones. The system might work something like this: An administrative assistant or clerical worker could only access e-mail. A middle manager could use e-mail, newsgroups, and the Web but could not enter chat channels. Only executives could access all Internet functions.

## DISCOVERIES FOR THE ADDICTED WORKER

When employees realize they have become addicted to the Internet and seek help to regulate their usage, they can take the opportunity to explore their possible motivations for diving into chat rooms or MUDs on the job and appropriately rechannel that energy. As a worker hooked on the Net, perhaps you're avoiding work for half the day because you simply don't like your job and want to escape from it and the negative feelings you associate with it. Consider your actions as a cue that it's time to seriously pursue a new job or even launch a new career.

If you find yourself complaining about your boss or work environment in your personal e-mail messages, maybe you need to start addressing those issues directly in the workplace. Or if you're finding trusted confidants only in chat rooms, perhaps you can identify a coworker whom you can approach with your discontent so you can get a reality check or even gain an ally. If you're gravitating to newsgroups during work time because you feel that you just don't fit in at your office, announce your desire to form an interest group in something you enjoy by posting a notice on your company's bulletin board.

The Internet looms as a potentially seductive force for anyone who has full access to it in the workplace, but not all employees get lost in cyberspace. Many workers send and receive only work-related e-mail, explore only those Web sites that relate to their company's mission, and steer clear of time-consuming detours into interactive domains. Others may indulge in an occasional e-mail to a friend no more often than they would make a personal phone call on company time, while otherwise refraining from abuse of Internet privileges. If you're the one person in your work team of four who has gone surfin' every day on the job, it doesn't make you wrong, nor does it mean you're not a good worker. More likely, your divergence signals that something in your life may be unfulfilled and needs your attention.

## AN INTERNET CODE OF CONDUCT

Many of the work-related problems we've been discussing could be avoided if employers were clear about what was expected and allowed of their workers regarding Internet usage from the start. Rapid job dismissals for Internet abuse without issuance of specific guidelines for Net use, or the lack of a warning at the first sign of deviant on-line activity, is not fair to workers. Such a hard-line response creates a climate of fear, distrust, and resentment in the workplace that will undermine productivity and cooperation even among those workers who have not gone off surfin.'

But most employers have yet to catch on to this side of the Internet story. In their bottom-line vision of profits and productivity, they have recognized only one major need regarding the Internet and their workers: make sure their employees know how to use the Internet. As the Internet quickly moves toward becoming a workplace norm, it's time to expand that vision. Employers must realize that they also need a clear set of rules and policies governing Internet usage to ensure that everyone will approach the Internet with a common understanding.

Not many have moved in this direction yet. One survey of executives revealed that less than a third had adopted any official policy for Internet use. Whether you're running a company large or small, don't lag behind. Whether you're about to introduce the Internet to your employees or whether you've floundered without specific Net guidelines for months or even years, it's time to adopt an Internet Code of Conduct. Here's one potential code to follow, excerpted from guidelines suggested by The Society for Human Resource Management (used by permission):

*Statement of purpose—Access to the Internet has been provided to staff members for the benefit of the organization* and its customers. *To ensure that all employees are responsible, productive Internet users who protect the company's public image, the following guidelines have been established for using the Internet:*

*Acceptable uses of the Internet—Employees accessing the Internet are representing the company. All communications should be for professional reasons. Employees are responsible for seeing that the Internet is used in an effective, ethical, and lawful manner. Internet Relay chat channels may be used only to conduct official company business, or to gain technical or analytical advice. Databases may be accessed for information as needed. E-mail may be used for business contacts.*

*Unacceptable use of the Internet—The Internet should not be used for personal gain or advancement of individual views. Solicitation of noncompany business, or any use of the Internet for personal gain is strictly prohibited. Use of the Internet must not disrupt the operation of the company network or the networks of others. It must not interfere with your productivity.*

*Communications—Each employee is responsible for the content of all text, audio, or images that they place or send over the Internet. Fraudulent, harassing, or obscene messages are prohibited. All messages communicated on the Internet should have your name attached. No messages will be transmitted under an assumed name. Users may not attempt to obscure the origin of any message. Information published on the Internet should not violate or infringe upon the rights of others. No abusive, profane, or offensive language is to be transmitted through the system. Employees who wish to express personal opinions on the Internet are encouraged to obtain their own usernames on other Internet systems.*

*Security—All messages created, sent, or retrieved over the Internet are the property of the company and should be considered public information. The company reserves the right to access and monitor all messages and files on the computer*

*screen as deemed necessary and appropriate. Internet mes-*
*sages are public communication and are not private. All*
*communications including text and images can be disclosed*
*to law enforcement or other third parties without prior con-*
*sent of the sender or receiver.*

*Violations—Violations of any guidelines listed here may*
*result in disciplinary action up to and including termina-*
*tion.*

I recommend that employers issue a copy of these guidelines to any worker with Internet access and require the worker's signature indicating understanding and acceptance of the code. When violations occur, employees should have a right to expect a three-tiered response: a warning at the first offense, a suspension the second time, and dismissal for the third offense—unless extreme circumstances such as deliberately misrepresenting the company warrant an immediate firing. And at the first two checkpoints, employers should take appropriate opportunities to educate and inform a worker in violation of the code about Internet addiction and to steer interested employees to sources for help.

By adopting this code or developing one like it, employers demonstrate a responsible and aware attitude toward the Internet and encourage a responsible approach by their workers. It may be impossible to accurately foresee the long-term growth of the Internet as a popular workplace tool, but with business and political leaders throughout the world strongly promoting the Net as a major source of international trade, it's even more important to be prepared. With clear guidelines for Internet use, employer and employee alike at least can move toward the new century together with a common understanding of how they'll handle it. In a work world clouded by uncertainty and marred by divisions, that would represent a major accomplishment.

## NINE

# Staying on Track

*Finding the trigger and stopping it is the key, because where the Internet is concerned, once you're in it, you're really in it.* —TONYA, A 23-YEAR-OLD COMPUTER ENGINEER

et's pause for a moment and look back to survey the damages caused by Internet addiction. Lost jobs. College expulsions. Teenagers breaking down. Families in crisis. Pedophiles stalking kids. Marriages destroyed. Domestic violence unchecked. Deepening depression. Heightened anxiety. Mounting debts. Broken trust. Secrets, lies, and cover-ups.

It's true that when you consider the entire worldwide population of Internet users, these examples may represent an extreme. Many people are turning to the Internet for useful purposes without getting hooked on the Net's alluring interactive features—so far anyway. But as we've seen, the progression from casual and appropriate usage, to time-consuming annoyance, to disturbing obsession, to extreme behavior and resultant upheaval moves swiftly and almost invisibly. And in my experience communicating with hundreds who have tumbled into a dark cyberabyss, it's only when Internet users reach the extreme edge of aberrant behavior and major turmoil that they'll step into the light, admit to what's happened, and look for help.

Don't make the same mistake. Don't wait, as they say in other addiction circles, until you hit rock bottom before recognizing how the Internet may be impacting your life and the lives of those you love. Don't reach the brink of getting fired, flunking out of school, divorcing your spouse, or plotting to run away from home before seeking assistance and charting a new course. Don't ignore the evidence of the negative consequences that already may stand before you.

When I remember back to the original questionnaire I posted on the Internet to determine whether people really were becoming addicted to it, one of the more disturbing and revealing results emerged in answer to this question: *Do you continue to use the Internet excessively despite significant problems it may be causing in your real life?* Sixty-eight percent of those initial respondents said yes! Why would those using the Internet keep adding to the turmoil it already was creating? Why did they continue to sabotage themselves?

People from all points of cyberspace tend to reject any notion that something with the serious connotation of addiction can apply to the Internet, a seemingly positive technological development. The denial is strong. The psychological dependence on the numbing or happy feelings experienced on-line leaves a deep imprint. The excitement that comes with the newness of a different experience has not even worn off yet. Problems are blamed on someone or something else.

But perhaps the most striking reason I've observed as to why Internet users keep on surfing despite the negative consequences is this: Obsessive Internet users innocently and honestly believe their Net-related problems will only be temporary. After all, the problems just arrived in their lives so, Internet users assume, they'll leave as quickly as they came on. If my grades shot down in one semester, they can vault back up next semester with just a little adjustment of my Net habits. If my boss got suspi-

cious about my wanderings down the information superhighway this week, I'll cool it a bit and be back in her or
his good graces by next week. If I'm losing sleep now, I
can catch up on the weekend. If my husband complains
about my on-line flirting today, he'll find something new
to complain about tomorrow.

It's understandable that you might blind yourself to
the long-term negative consequences of your Internet
habits. Everything that happens on the Net can seem
fleeting, and besides, compared with other sources of potential addiction, the Internet itself has such a short history that we don't easily associate anything long-term
with it. When you see studies conducted on the physio-
logical effects of a 30-year smoking habit, or the behavioral implications of watching TV excessively from early
childhood to midlife, you find no parallel association
with the Internet. Who knows the long-term effects of
getting lost in cyberspace? What appears to be a problem
today could be the norm tomorrow, you reason. And
maybe the Internet will fade from the spotlight as quickly
as CB radio, and all the problems will slip away along with
a general decline in interest.

The trap in this reasoning is that no matter how swiftly
negative consequences of Internet addiction sweep into
your life, the damages left behind can last long after the
Internet has faded from the focal point of your existence
or even from its status as technological wonder of the
new century. The harm from a few weeks or months of
obsessive Internet use still could be with you months or
years later. Divorces are final. Losing jobs today could
mean a long phase of unemployment. So if you have
heard yourself or the Internet user in your life deflect attention from a Net habit because any problems caused by
it simply won't last, it's time to take a fresh look at this
line of thinking.

## *Consider the Long-Term Consequences*

If you're using the Internet today and you've recognized one or more of the problems we've been discussing in the previous chapters, or someone in your life is trying to alert you to the real-life trouble you're causing, look more closely at the negative consequences involved. Think about those consequences in the months ahead. Ask yourself these questions:

■ *Whom are you hurting?* If your partner, parents, children, boyfriend, girlfriend, or best friend tells you that your behavior on the Internet is bringing them grief, listen to what they say. Even if you believe your Net habits have not yet affected you personally, if they're impacting others close to you, then your relationships are suffering. Do you really want to go on hurting your loved ones while risking divorce or family strife? Are the kicks you get from a cyberfling or chat-room socializing really worth the long-term fallout?

■ *Where will you be in your work or school life one year down the road?* If your boss has "busted" you once already for spending company time on personal Internet use and issued a warning, what's likely to happen if you don't change? Do you really want to lose this job, and if you do get fired, are you prepared to launch a new job search with this blemish on your record? If you're in college, what's going to happen if you do flunk out? Are you ready to support yourself? Won't you miss college after you're gone?

■ *Where can you find greater rewards for your time, effort, and energy?* Internet addicts say they love the camaraderie of a large newsgroup or lively chat room, or the mental stimulation of endless reams of information on the Web, or the sense of achievement of mastering a MUD. But will any of those payoffs stick? Remember how easily a new friend or cyberlover can blip off the screen and out of your life. Open your eyes to the investments you can make in your real life to build relationships and create joy and happiness that will last.

■ *Who were you before this new obsession, and do you really want to continue to lose that person?* So many Internet addicts tell me they were honest, dependable, and conscientious before they fell into their Net habits and resulting personality changes. Do you really want to be seen by those in your life as undependable, uncaring, and unavailable for help, support, and close human contact? While you're getting caught up in your new on-line personas and reveling in the easy intimacy in the faceless community, don't forget to check in with the best parts of you that you might be leaving behind.

■ *Do you really want to be wasting so much time?* When using the Internet begins to consume vast blocks of time, you may react with surprise or embarrassment, or maybe you're having too much fun to pay attention at all. Back up a minute. First, ask if you really want to be wasting time on a new diversion, no matter how alluring. Is such a practice consistent with your life goals? Is it helping you get where you want to go? Are you wasteful and frivolous in other aspects of your life? Think about how to bring your Internet usage into alignment with what you believe and value.

Once you get more clear on the negative long-term consequences of your obsessive Internet usage, you will become more strongly motivated to moderate your habits. That's when you'll stand a better chance of successfully utilizing the time-management techniques and other recovery strategies I've outlined. Still, you may find yourself self-conscious about trying to adopt a recovery strategy to combat something you do on the computer as if it were an addictive substance. Even in professional psychological or psychiatric circles, use of the word *addiction* stirs so much debate that a serious outlook and response to Internet-related problems can be undermined.

## A Chemical Response to Addictive Behavior?

The problem stems from a lack of agreement among professionals on what constitutes an addiction. The common argument is that we can be addicted only to physical substances to which we have a chemical response in our bodies. If our bodies are hooked, we're hooked. Well, recent scientific evidence suggests that it may be possible to experience habit-forming chemical reactions to behavior as well as to substances. Scientists studying the effect of addictions on the brain have focused new attention on dopamine, a substance in the brain associated with pleasure and elation. Scientists believe that levels of dopamine may rise not only from drinking alcohol or taking drugs, but from gambling, eating chocolate, or even from receiving a hug or word of praise. And when something makes our dopamine level rise, we naturally want more of it. Another study indicated that as our brain reacts to familiar stimuli it can alter our behavior without our ever really knowing it, which may explain our tendency to excessively repeat addictive patterns.

So do some Internet users aggressively and persistently chase those positive feelings they experience online because of a chemical reaction in the brain? Can we be getting so mesmerized by the Internet's words and images on our computer screens that they begin to alter how we act in ways that we don't notice while they're happening? It is too early to draw such broad conclusions, but these new studies clearly point to addictive responses to feelings and experiences we get from something we ingest or something we do, rather than an addiction to the substance itself. Again, remind yourself that you're not addicted to the Internet per se, you're hooked on a certain emotional and perhaps even mental response you get from your on-line practices. In this light, getting hooked on the Internet makes as much sense as getting hooked on gambling.

But whether you accept the term Internet addiction or prefer calling it compulsive computer behavior, don't get so caught up in semantics or debates that you lose sight of the basic facts. You've got a problem with how you're using the Internet and you need to do something about it. And it *is* possible to change. Many Internet users have made major adjustments in the amount of time they devote to the Net and how they use it. Where my e-mail box used to be filled with nothing but distress signals from Internet addicts, or more likely from their loved ones, I now hear a bit more frequently from those who proudly share how they have regained control over their Internet habits and their lives.

## ONE MARRIAGE SAVED

Mick had been married to Andrea for almost 25 years when he caught her engaging in cyberaffairs. She inadvertently had left two incoming e-mail messages from her on-line lovers on the computer screen when she went out one morning, and Mick discovered them. He insisted they enter counseling together, and Andrea agreed. They were fortunate enough to work with a counselor who, despite Andrea's denial, recognized that she was addicted to her cyberlove experiences. He compared it to alcoholism and urged her to stop and even attend AA meetings. The counselor also pinpointed general communications problems in the marriage and helped both Andrea and Mick learn to express their feelings to one another more freely and honestly.

When Mick first e-mailed me, he wanted to know whether Andrea needed to give up the Internet entirely, as their counselor recommended, or would it be enough if she stopped fooling around with men and strictly limited her other on-line endeavors? I advised him that giving up the Internet completely would lead to major withdrawal symptoms for Andrea, and that moderating her use, with Mick actively assisting and supporting her efforts, could help rebuild trust between them. And I urged him to continue in counseling together. Three months later, Mick sent me this e-mail update:

"Therapy has been very helpful for us. We continue to get better at sharing and expressing our feelings, both good and bad. Andrea still chats with her local girlfriends, but she gave up all her male 'buddies' and her usage is about a 10th of what it was. I feel that as long as she remains faithful to me in cyberspace and real life, then our relationship will be healthy. And I have access to her password now, which shows how much more open and honest she is about the Internet. I think sometimes she left those messages on the screen because she wanted to get caught so we would get help in our marriage. Our therapist is amazed at the goodwill we have shown toward each other and believes our marriage is much better than most and has the potential to be stronger than it ever was. We're getting ready to go away together to celebrate our 25th wedding anniversary!"

Andrea's success in giving up her cyberaffairs and regulating her on-line usage dispels those harsh admonishments Internet addicts often hear to "Get a life!" As one recovering Internet addict cleverly put it: "Getting a life is not the solution. Getting a life is really the problem. Chat-room addicts have made for themselves a virtual life in which they have friends who are warm, loving, caring people available any time of the day and night. That's not easy for anybody to give up."

To recover from Internet addiction, then, you want to work toward giving up the life you turned to in cyberspace. As you let go, you want to reclaim your life as it was before you went wandering through cyberspace. You also want to think in terms of rediscovering the possibilities for improving the circumstances in your life, as Andrea did in strengthening her marriage with Mick. You want to create a more solid balance in your life that may include limited Internet use within an overall context of healthy relationships, emotional awareness, and diverse interests and activities. Here are a few more pointers to help guide you on your way toward staying on track.

### RECOVERY STRATEGY 19:
*Five Tips for the Journey of Recovery*

1. *Avoid relapsing.* Recovering from any addiction carries the risk of relapsing. I find that most Internet addicts who relapse have deviated from their new schedule that incorporates brief but regular periods of on-line use. Review the section about scheduling limited Internet time into your weekly routine, as outlined in Recovery Strategy 3 in Chapter 2. Once you decide on a schedule, keep to it for at least three weeks before attempting to make any necessary minor changes. In working to create new and healthier habits, you're aiming for consistency.

2. *Be patient with yourself.* When Internet addicts first awaken to the severe problems their habit has triggered,

they often panic and decide to quit cold turkey. Then, when hit with withdrawal, they rush back to their same Net patterns and fall into a stop/start cycle that's difficult to break. Even those who understand that moderation is a more appropriate goal for Internet addiction tend to get impatient when their spouse keeps pestering them to stop or their schoolwork still seems overwhelming. Give it time. Real-life change takes longer than the instant intimacy and satisfaction you're used to from the Net.

3. *Give yourself credit for trying.* It's natural to feel embarrassed or ashamed that you got hooked on the Internet and you can't seem to handle the problem overnight. But acknowledge yourself for recognizing the issue and setting out to address it at all. You're already well ahead of the cultural curve in your response to this new phenomenon. If you gave up a favorite chat room or MUD, or you cut your e-mail time in half, understand that you have taken major strides. Emphasize what you have accomplished in your moderation efforts, not the goals you haven't yet achieved.

4. *Tune in to your addictive triggers.* Review Recovery Strategy 5, Recognize Your Addictive Triggers, from Chapter 3 and refer to it whenever you feel the threat of your Net habits spinning out of control again. Those choice points are critical. If you can stop before going on-line and recognize the emotion fueling your behavior, you have the opportunity to give yourself a different message and make a new choice every time. Life is all about choices, and when you're aware of what you're choosing and why, you stand a better chance of making wiser decisions.

5. *Get your loved ones on board.* The support of your partner or other loved one can aid your recovery signifi-

cantly. Just as that person recognized the damage caused by your excessive Internet use more readily than you did, he or she also can see and speak to the progress you're making and help keep you motivated to change. If your partner has acted in codependent ways in the past, urge him or her to read books about this subject, such as *Codependent No More* by Melody Beattie. Also, make sure that your loved one agrees that your goal is moderation, not abstinence. You need to be on the same page. You may want to work with your loved one to decide on your new goals.

## LOCATING OUTSIDE HELP

Even with the strong support of loved ones, regaining control of your Internet habits can be difficult to take on alone. At some point, you probably will want to at least consider seeking outside help. An addiction treatment program, a therapist or counselor who understands Internet addiction, or a good support group can help keep you on track. But how do you find one?

Treatment programs that specifically address Internet addiction are only slowly beginning to emerge. That's why I developed the Center for On-Line Addiction. The center provides personal consultation and supportive counseling for Internet addicts and their families. It also maintains updated listings of mental health clinics specializing in Internet addiction to help you locate other knowledgeable professionals.

One such clinic is The Institute for Addiction Recovery at Proctor Hospital in Peoria, Illinois, which launched a Computer/Internet Addiction Service in 1996. "We were one of the first gambling addiction programs when no one was taking that issue seriously," said Ed Falhbeck, the Institute's marketing representative. "When we started to see cases of people addicted to the Internet, we expanded into this new area." So far, most treatment has followed the addiction abstinence model and has been conducted on an outpatient basis.

Dr. Maressa Hecht Orzack recognized the same need and founded the Computer Addiction Services at McLean Hospital in Belmont, Massachusetts. She described one recent case of working with a graduate student whose chat-room habits were undermining his attempt to finish his dissertation. In helping him moderate his usage and stay on track to earn his Ph.D., Dr. Hecht Orzack helped the student establish a new schedule of one hour of work followed by a half hour of recreation, which he was free to spend exercising, calling friends, or chatting on the Internet.

Clinicians or administrators of addiction treatment programs contact me to inquire about my research as they consider treatment approaches for those who come to them with Internet-triggered problems. The Alberta (Canada) Alcohol and Drug Abuse Commission sought information from me in response to the case of a teenage boy who had dropped out of school after becoming obsessed with the Net's interactive games. Those who treat various addictions watch for emerging trends in the field, so new or expanded programs designed to assist Internet addicts may begin to surface rapidly as this book and other research and reports of the problem become more widely circulated. In Chapter 7, I mentioned two new Internet addiction programs at college counseling centers. With so much research in this realm emanating from universities, similar programs likely will sprout up soon.

Don't assume that you can get help only from those few Internet addiction treatment programs already out there. Contact any addiction treatment facilities in your area and ask whether they're familiar with Internet addiction and how they would treat it. If you don't like what you hear, focus your search on finding a good individual therapist.

When interviewing potential therapists, inquire about their knowledge of the Internet and whether they believe people really can get addicted to using it. If they don't know much about the makings of the Internet now, are they at least willing to learn more about it from you and other sources? And will they agree to goals of helping you identify the triggers for your excessive usage and assist you in moderating your on-line time? While obtaining answers to these questions, don't forget the other important considerations of choosing a therapist for any reason: Do you feel comfortable with the therapist and confident in his or her ability and judgment? Can you work with the therapist as a team focused on your problems?

## A Creative Counseling Approach

Tonya, a 23-year-old computer engineer in Brooklyn, recommends therapy to all her friends whose lives have spun out of control from excessive Internet use. She tells them how well it worked for her. While still a student three years ago, Tonya became first an Internet chat-room junkie, then quickly added newsgroups to her growing Net repertoire. We know from the many examples in Chapter 7 how Internet addiction in college can impact grades, and Tonya soon wound up on probation. This threw her into a major depression, and she sought counseling. She found someone she could trust and in time learned that she, like many others we've seen, was using the Net to escape from a depression she already had.

"Finding the trigger and stopping it is the key," says Tonya, "because where the Internet is concerned, once you're in it, you're really in."

She cut her Net time down from more than 40 hours per week to about 15 hours, and as her Internet time went down her grades bounced back up. But she still found herself lapsing into occasional Internet binges and strategized with her therapist to find stronger control methods. They both agreed that investing several hours on one weekend day was not a problem, and they set a goal of one hour per evening on weeknights. But when Tonya exceeded that limit, she felt guilty and more depressed. So her therapist took what psychologists might call a paradoxical approach. She told Tonya that she now had full permission to stay on the Net for *two* full hours every night.

To her surprise, Tonya learned that having full permission to stay on longer actually made it easier for her to go back to her initial schedule and even trim her time further; she no longer had to fight against her guilt or kick herself for failing to stick to more rigid standards. After graduating in good standing and landing a job, Tonya became a strong proponent of professional counseling.

"I know that psychotherapy is not for everyone, but I believe anyone considering that route should give it a try," Tonya urges. "That goes for anyone who believes successful therapy is impossible for some reason, or they're too young or something."

## SUPPORT GROUPS, OFF-LINE AND ON

If individual therapy just doesn't fit for you, or you've been unable to find a counselor who seems right, you may want to seek a support group. Of course, just as you won't find many clinics specifically geared to treating Internet addiction, you won't find many support groups for on-lineaholics either. Don't despair. You may benefit from attending a support group centered on other kinds of addictive behavior, such as gambling or eating disorders. In listening to the sharing in such a group, you may gain important insight into the origins of your own addictive patterns of behavior and gain support in taking control of your life through regulating your Internet usage.

Contact your local mental health center or drug and alcohol rehabilitation center for leads. When checking out a possible support group, use many of the same criteria you followed in searching for a therapist. Do you feel comfortable in that group's environment? Do members appear welcoming to you and your problems with the Internet? Do you believe that members will understand your goals and validate your efforts to reach them? In asking the right questions when evaluating a group, you may even be led to others who are wrestling with the same problems and you may find yourself part of a newly forming group just for Internet addicts.

An Internet addiction support group was formed more than two years ago on the Internet itself. Although launched as a joke, many enlisting members exchanged serious messages about the negative consequences they encountered from their excessive on-line usage and shared ideas for coping strategies. Tonya visited the on-line group to offer to follow up with anyone interested in hearing about her experiences in therapy. She didn't get many takers.

The problem with support groups on the Net is that you're not apt to find much structure or consistency. Remember, this is the unregulated Internet—anyone can join, no one's in control, anything goes. One day a sincere discussion about real problems of excessive use draws input from four or five people making legitimate efforts to cut back. The next day all visitors to the group are engaged in a one-upmanship battle over the most creative list that begins: "You Know You Are Addicted to the Internet When. . . ." Typical entries include "Your eyeglasses have a Web site burned in on them," "You wonder how your service provider is allowed to call 200 hours per month unlimited," or "You start putting sideways smiley faces when you write your friends real notes."

## SPOUSES OR FAMILY MEMBERS: WHERE TO TURN?

Spouses, parents, and other loved ones of an Internet addict also may need outside support, especially if the on-lineaholic remains in denial of the problem. If you're swimming in the turmoil caused by your loved one's addiction, you may believe that no one understands how you feel or what you're experiencing. Your friends who don't know much about the Internet may stare at you in disbelief when you announce that your spouse or child is addicted to the Net. They may accuse you of exaggerating, masking other problems, or just failing to get in step with the times. Beyond seeking help for the Internet addict in your life, you need help for yourself.

Look for family support groups for other addictions, such as Al-Anon. Contact your local AA chapter or community mental health center to learn where to turn and what you might expect. For starters, you'll receive literature outlining the issues of dealing with any addiction in the family. If you attend meetings, just listen to the experience of family members of alcoholics and see where they resonate with your situation. As a spouse, simply hearing the anger and frustration of other spouses living with addiction under their roof can help you feel validated and less alone. You may also find others living close to someone's Internet Addiction and form your own informal support group. A woman in Scotland, whose husband had cultivated an 18-hour daily Internet habit and begun a cyberaffair, set up a support group for spouses of

Internet addicts. Before long, the group had 20 members!

If you're a parent of a child hooked on the Net, talk to your child's teacher or contact your local Parents Association and explain what you're experiencing. You may find other parents going through similar frustrations with whom you can meet informally for mutual guidance and support. You also might strategize together on how to educate officials in your school district about this new threat to children's well-being and the role their schools may be playing inadvertently.

## USING PERSONAL EXPERIENCE TO REACH ADDICTED SISTER

Becky wants to help her sister Yolanda regain control over a severe Internet habit. Married nine years with an eight-year-old daughter and a two-year-old son, Yolanda spends 60 hours per week in chat rooms. She's hiding her Visa bills for on-line service bills from her husband, who's often away weekends on National Guard duty. She sold her new car when she couldn't afford to make the payments and bought an old clunker that barely runs. Now she's met a guy on-line and is planning to leave her husband to run off with him. Becky knows the story all too well. Until a year ago, she lived it herself.

"I'm so very scared for her, but she's just like how I used to be—in denial," explains Becky. "I call her up at 2 P.M. on a Saturday or Sunday and wake her up. I hear her kids running around, and God knows how long they've been unsupervised. She wants to sell her house to be near this other addict who lives 300 miles away, and the guy's only 21 with no job!"

Becky is a former chat-room addict. In fact, she originally had turned her sister on to the same group she fre-

quented. Becky left her own husband to be with her cyberlover, but soon after her marriage dissolved she woke
up to the destructive role of the Internet in her world.
She held on to a new job as a developer of Web pages,
but otherwise she doesn't go near the Net. Now she's
hoping to help Yolanda through a family intervention
that also would include Yolanda's husband. Becky is
hopeful that her voice will get through to her addicted
sister. After all, Becky reasons, she speaks from the voice
of authority.

Whether you're the Internet addict seeking to recover
and regain control or you're the partner or parent, you'll
find that those who have shared your experience most directly will be especially willing to help in any way they
can. Recognition of Internet addiction and recovery
from it, in this respect, has been very much a grassroots
effort so far. Just as those who caught on early to the benefits and pleasures of using the Internet passed the word
eagerly to their family, friends, and coworkers, those who
now understand Internet addiction from firsthand experience, or from hearing about someone near them, have
begun to spread the news about the darker side of cyberspace. If you look for this growing grapevine, you'll probably find it.

Still, as an Internet addict seeking your own path to
recovery, ultimate responsibility for regaining control lies
in your own hands. You must decide what goals to set for
moderating your Internet usage and finding a balance in
your life again. You also must determine when you've
achieved recovery.

That may sound simple, but I've found that for Internet addicts this task constitutes one of the more challenging recovery steps. With alcoholism, recovery is more
straightforward. By definition, you always will be a recovering alcoholic. Each day that you maintain sobriety, you
have met your primary goal, and your success path is

marked by anniversary dates of your first day sober. So without such a clear-cut structure, how do you know if and when you're recovering from Internet addiction? Only you can say, but here are some general checkpoints to assist you.

## RECOVERY STRATEGY 20:
### *Tune in to the Signs of Recovery*

1. You stick to your schedule of Internet use and don't eclipse your targeted number of total hours on-line each week.
2. Your partner, parent, or other loved one tells you they see the difference in your Internet habits and your behavior toward them.
3. You keep a strict accounting of the money you spend for on-line service fees and stay within your budget.
4. You perform work tasks, school assignments, or household chores in a timely fashion that closely resembles your pattern before turning to addictive Internet use.
5. You rediscover those favorite hobbies and activities you used to enjoy.
6. You expend greater energy communicating with those directly in front of you than to strangers on the Net.
7. You see others obsessed with the Internet in a different light, with an understanding that they're creating problems for themselves and those closest to them.
8. When you do use the Internet for legitimate reasons or for your limited entertainment slots, you feel less and less tempted to resume your old habits.

9.  You feel a greater desire to go out with your loved ones and socialize with friends, turning down fewer invitations and making more of your own.
10. You look back at your time of addiction to the Internet and see a different person from a different time.

## GET PEOPLE TALKING

As you move further along in your own recovery, or you gain greater awareness and support for your role as the loved one of an Internet addict, you can do yourself and others a service by joining in the emerging dialogue about this worldwide phenomenon. Talk about what's happened to you and what you've learned. Compare notes with others. Urge professionals in addiction treatment centers or counselors to pay more attention to this problem. Get those at work and school to address the issues that you raise.

If you've been unfortunate enough to become part of the problem of Internet addiction, you now have the opportunity to be part of the broader solution. You can become one of the global messengers for change in how we view the Internet and what we need to understand about its more alluring features. The Internet, when properly used, really can represent the cutting edge of progress. But when you encourage a greater dialogue about the potential pitfalls of excessive Internet use, you're on the equally important cutting edge of awareness about something apparently destined to become part of almost all our lives. And soon.

# Epilogue

This book not only culminates my clinical research but also represents an important first step toward further discovery. I have already seen the gates of progress open as colleagues have joined me in studying the psychological aspects of the Internet. At the 1997 American Psychological Association's (APA) annual convention in Chicago, several academic papers and symposia presented research and theories on the effects of on-line behavior patterns. These included a general discussion of technological addictions, the incidence of pathological Internet use, identification of Internet dependency among college students, and the utility of psychotherapy on the Internet. The overflow attendance at these presentations demonstrated the growing demand among mental health professionals for knowledge about Internet use.

Serving on its editorial board, a new journal, *Cyber-Psychology and Behavior*, has recently been launched to address Internet use and addiction. Practitioners have also founded Computer/Internet Addiction Recovery Centers. It is possible that with years of collective effort, Internet dependence may be recognized as a legitimate impulse-control disorder worthy of its own classification in future revisions of the American Psychiatric Association's *Diagnostic and Statistical Manual of Mental Disorders*. Until then, it is my hope that the worldwide body of professionals and laypeople alike will recognize and respond to the reality of Internet addiction and to the threat of its rapid expansion.

It is essential to gain a better understanding of the underlying motivations of Internet addiction. Future research should focus on how psychiatric illness such as depression or bipolar disorder play a role in the development of pathological Internet use. Longitudinal studies of Internet users with heavy usage patterns may reveal how personality traits, family dynamics, or communication skills influence the way people utilize the Internet. Researchers should also undertake outcome studies to determine the efficacy of various forms of therapy and to compare these outcomes with the more traditional methods of recovery. Finally, the legal implications of this phenomenon need to be explored. I have been asked to serve as an expert witness in divorce suits and custody battles that have resulted from a spouse's excessive Internet use. And this trend is likely to continue. For more information on current trends in the field of Internet addiction, please contact the Center for On-Line Addiction at its Web site at http://www.netaddiction.com.

# Notes

## Introduction: A Controversial New Addiction

*Page 3:* Diagnostic criteria for Internet addiction adapted from criteria used to define Substance Dependence/Pathological Gambling from the American Psychiatric Association (1995). *Diagnostic and Statistical Manual of Mental Disorders.* 4th ed. Washington, D.C.: Author.

*Page 6:* Steven Levy, "Breathing Is Also Addictive," *Newsweek,* Dec. 30, 1996/Jan. 6, 1997, 52–53.

## Chapter 1 The Dark Side of Cyberspace

*Page 27:* Press Release, latest survey report by IntelliQuest Information Group, Inc. of Austin, TX. November 17, 1997, page 1.

## Chapter 3 Profiles of On-lineaholics

*Page 87:* Adapted from Patrick Fanning and John T. O'Neill; *The Addiction Workbook: A Step-by-Step Guide to Quitting Alcohol and Drugs* (Oakland, CA: New Harbinger Publications, Inc., 1996), 11–14.

## Chapter 4 The Faceless Community

*Page 105:* Sherry Turkle, *Life on the Screen: Identity in the Age of the Internet* (New York: Simon & Schuster, 1995), 30.

CHAPTER 5 CYBERWIDOWS:
VICTIMS OF TERMINAL LOVE

*Page 135:* Abigail Trafford, *Crazy Time: Surviving Divorce* (New York: Bantam, 1982), 164–65.

CHAPTER 6 PARENTS, KIDS,
AND A TECHNOLOGICAL TIME BOMB

*Page 146:* M. J. Andersen, "Info Age: Teen Cyberlove Just a New Version of an Old Problem," *Providence Journal-Bulletin,* 26 April 1997.

*Page 146:* Kim Bell, "A Fatal On-Line Attraction," *St. Louis Post-Dispatch,* 6 October 1996, p. 1.

*Page 147:* Rajiv Chandrasekaran, "Protecting Children's Privacy Online," *The Washington Post,* 14 June 1997, p. D1.

*Page 147:* Around the Nation, "AOL Found Not Liable for Pornography." *The Washington Post,* 15 June 1997, p. A15.

*Page 147:* Harry Lewis, "Other Girls Enticed Over Net: Police," *The Philadelphia Inquirer,* 21 February 1997, p. R1.

*Page 158:* Who Knew? "SOS for Surfaholics," *Seventeen,* July 1997, 52.

*Page 164:* C. McNamara, "Tracking the Cyberspace Predator," *Reader's Digest,* November 1995, 109.

*Page 165:* John M. Broder, "White House Is Set to Ease Its Stance on Internet Smut," *The New York Times,* 16 June 1997, p. A1.

*Page 166:* Susan D. Haas, "Parents—Beware of Flashers in Cyberspace," *The Buffalo News,* 11 February 1997, p. D7.

*Page 166:* Ibid.

*Page 170:* Marie Winn, *The Plug-In Drug* (New York: Viking Penguin, Inc., 1977), 148.

*Page 170:* Ibid., 146.

*Page 172:* Antonia Barber, "Net's Educational Value Questioned," *USA Today,* 11 March 1997, p. 4D.

## CHAPTER 7 FRATERNITIES OF NETHEADS

*Page 176:* Karen Brady, "Dropout Rise a Net Result of Computers," *The Buffalo News,* 21 April 1996, p. A1.

## CHAPTER 8 NO WORK TODAY — EVERYBODY'S GONE SURFIN'

*Page 195:* Press release, "Surf's Up! Is Productivity Down?" *Robert Half International,* 10 October 1996, p. 1.

*Page 195:* Sharon Machlis, "Gotcha! Monitoring Tools Track Web Surfing at Work." *Computerworld,* 7 April 1997, p. 2.

*Page 212:* Ellen Neuborne, "Bosses Worry Net Access Will Cut Productivity," *USA Today,* 16 April 1997, p. 4B.

*Page 212:* This excerpt from "Sample Internet Policy" has been provided as a professional courtesy by the Society for Human Resource Management, 1800 Duke Street, Alexandria, VA.

## CHAPTER 9 STAYING ON TRACK

*Page 220:* N. D. Volkow, G. J. Wang, M. W. Fischman, R. W. Voltin, J. S. Fowler, N. N. Abumred, S. Vitkun, J. Logan, S. J. Gatley, N. Pappas, R. Hyitzman, and L. E. Shey. "Relationship between Subjective Effect of Cocaine and Dopamine Transporter Occupancy." *Nature* 386 (April 24, 1997):827–30 and N. D. Volkow, G. J. Wang, J. S. Fowler, J. Logan, S. J. Gatley, R. Hyitzman, A. D. Chen, S. L. Dewey, and N. Pappas. "Decreased Striatal Dopamanergic Responsiveness in Detoxified Cocaine-Dependent Species." *Nature* 386 (April 24, 1997):830–33.

*Page 220:* G. S. Berns, J. D. Cohen, and M. A. Mintun. "Brain Regions Responsive to Novelty in the Absence of Awareness." *Science* 276, no. 5316 (1997):1272–76.

*Page 230:* Kimberley A. Strassel, "Caught in the Web: This Computer Virus Might Ruin Your Life." *Wall Street Journal Europe,* 20 May 1996, p. 1.

# Bibliography

Abbott, D. A. "Pathological Gambling and the Family: Practical Implications," *Families in Society* 76, no. 4 (1995):213–19.

American Psychiatric Association. *Diagnostic and Statistical Manual of Mental Disorders*. 4th ed. Washington, DC: Author, 1995.

Andersen, M. J. "Info Age: Teen Cyberlove Just a New Version of an Old Problem." *Providence Journal-Bulletin*, 26 April 1997, p. A11.

Around the Nation. "AOL Found Not Liable for Pornography." *The Washington Post*, 15 June 1997, p. A15.

Barber, Antonia. "Net's Educational Value Questioned." *USA Today*, 11 March 1997, p. 4D.

Beck, Aaron, Fred D. Wright, Cory F. Newman, and Bruce S. Liese. *Cognitive Therapy of Substance Abuse*. New York, NY: Guilford Press, 1993.

Bell, K. "A Fatal Online Attraction." *St. Louis Post-Dispatch*, 6 October 1996, p. 1

Berns, G. S., J. D. Cohen, and M. A. Mintun. "Brain Regions Responsive to Novelty in the Absence of Awareness." *Science*. 276, no. 5316 (1997):1272–76.

Brady, Karen. "Dropout Rise a Net Result of Computers." *The Buffalo News*, 21 April 1996, p. A1.

Bristow-Braitman, A. "Addiction Recovery: Twelve Step Programs and Cognitive Behavioral Psychotherapy." *Journal of Counseling and Development* 73, no. 4 (1995):414–18.

Broder, John M. "White House is Set to Ease Its Stance on Internet Smut," *The New York Times*, 16 June 1997, p. A1.

Brownell, K. D., and C. G. Fairbirn. *Eating Disorders and Obesity: A Comprehensive Handbook.* New York, NY: Guilford Press, 1995.

Ceronk, T. "Co-Addiction as a Disease." *Psychiatric Annals* 21, no. 5 (1991):266–72.

Chandrasekaran, Rajiv. "Protecting Children's Privacy Online," *The Washington Post,* 14 June 1997, p. D1.

Cooper, M. L. "Parental Drinking Problems and Adolescent Offspring Substance Use: Moderating Effects of Demographic and Familial Factors." *Psychology of Addictive Behaviors.* 9, no. 1 (1995):36–52.

Dobson, K. S., ed. *Handbook of Cognitive-Behavioral Therapies.* New York, NY: Guilford Press, 1988, 95–96.

Domjan, M. *The Principles of Learning and Behavior.* 3rd ed. Pacific Grove, CA: Brooks/Cole, 1993.

Donovan, D., and G. A. Marlott. *Assessment of Addictive Behaviors.* New York: Guilford Press, 1988.

Dunlop, C., and R. Kling, eds. *Computerization and Controversy: Value Conflicts and Social Choices.* San Diego, CA: Academic Press, Inc., 1991.

Fanning, P. and J. T. O'Neill. *The Addiction Workbook: A Step-by-Step Guide to Quitting Alcohol and Drugs.* Oakland, CA: New Harbinger Publications, Inc., 1996.

Griffiths, M. "Technological Addictions." *Clinical Psychology Forum* 76 (1995):14–19.

Haas, Susan D. "Parents—Beware of Flashers in Cyberspace," *The Buffalo News,* 11 February 1997, p. D7.

Hester, R. K. *Handbook of Alcoholism Treatment Approaches: Effective Alternatives.* Boston, MA: Allyn & Bacon, 1993.

Huff, C., and T. Finhold. *Social Implications of Computing: Putting Computing in Its Place.* New York, NY: McGraw Hill, 1994.

Jones, S. G. CyberSociety: *Computer-Mediated Communication and Community.* Thousand Oaks, CA: Sage Publications, 1995.

Kanfer, F. H., and A. P. Goldstein, eds. *Helping People Change: A Textbook of Methods.* 4th ed. New York, NY: Pergamon Press, 1991.

Keepers, G. A. "Pathological Preoccupation with Video Games." *Journal of the American Academy of Child and Adolescent Psychiatry* 29, no. 1 (1990):49–50.

Kiesler, S., J. Siegel, and T. W. McGuire. "Social Psychological Aspects of Computer-Mediated Communication." *American Psychologist* 39, no. 10 (1984):1123–34.

Klebe-Trevino, L., and J. Webster. "Flow in Computer-Mediated Communication." *Communication Research* 19, no. 5 (1992): 539–73.

Lesieur, H. R., and S. B. Blume. "Pathological Gambling, Eating Disorders, and the Psychoactive Substance Use Disorders." *Journal of Addictive Diseases* 12, no. 3 (1993):89–102.

Levy, Steven. "Breathing Is Also Addictive," *Newsweek,* December 30/January 6, 1997, pp. 52–53.

Machlis, Sharon. "Gotcha! Monitoring Tools Track Web Surfing at Work." *Computerworld,* 4 April 1997, p. 1.

Martin, G., and J. Pear. *Behavior Modification: What It Is and How to Do It.* 4th ed. Englewood Cliffs, NJ: Prentice Hall, 1992.

McGurrin, M. C. *Pathological Gambling: Conceptual, Diagnostic, and Treatment Issues.* Sarasota, FL: Professional Research Press, 1992.

McNamara, C. "Tracking the Cyberspace Predator," *Reader's Digest,* November 1995, p. 109.

Meichenbaum, D. *Stress Inoculation Training.* New York, NY: Pergamon Press, 1985.

Neuborne, Ellen. "Bosses Worry Net Access Will Cut Productivity," *USA Today,* 16 April 1997, p. 4B.

Press Release, "Surf's Up! Is Productivity Down?" *Robert Half International,* 10 October 1996, p. 1.

Rheingold, H. *The Virtual Community: Homesteading on the Electronic Frontier.* Reading, MA: Addison-Wesley, 1993.

Riesmann, F. "What Makes an Effective Self-Help Group." *Self Help Reporter* 6 (1983):27–28.

Rosenberg, R. S. *The Social Implications of Computers.* Boston, MA: Academic Press, 1992.

Rushkoff, D. *Cyberia: Life in the Trenches of Hyperspace*. San Francisco: HarperSanFrancisco, 1994.

Scherer, K. "College Life Online: Healthy and Unhealthy Internet Use." *The Journal of College Student Development* (in press).

Shotton, M. "The Costs and Benefits of Computer Addiction." *Behaviour and Information Technology* 10, no. 3 (1991):219–30.

Snider, Mike "Growing On-line Population Making Internet 'Mass Media' " *USA Today*, 11 February 1997, p. 1.

Soper, B. W. "Junk-Time Junkies: An Emerging Addiction among Students." *School Counselor* 31, no. 1 (1983):40–43.

Strassel, Kimberley. "Caught in the Web: This Computer Virus Might Ruin Your Life." *Wall Street Journal Europe*, 20 May 1996, p. 1.

Thombs, D. L. *Introduction to Addictive Behaviors*. New York: Guilford Press, 1994.

Turkle, S. *The Second Self: Computers and the Human Spirit*. New York, NY: Simon & Schuster, 1984.

———. *Life on the Screen: Identity in the Age of the Internet*. New York, NY: Simon & Schuster, 1995.

Volkow, N. D., G. J. Wang, M. W. Fischman, R. W. Voltin, J. S. Fowler, N. N. Abumred, S. Vitkun, J. Logan, S. J. Gatley, N. Pappas, R. Hyitzman, and L. E. Shey. "Relationship between Subjective Effect of Cocaine and Dopamine Transporter Occupancy." *Nature* 386 (April 24, 1997):827–30.

Volkow, N. D., G. J. Wang, J. S. Fowler, J. Logan, S. J. Gatley, R. Hyitzman, A. D. Chen, S. L. Dewey, and N. Pappas. "Decreased Striatial Dopamanergic Responsiveness in Detoxified Cocaine-Dependent Species." *Nature* 386 (April 24, 1997):830–33.

Walters, G. D. "Drug-Seeking Behavior: Disease or Lifestyle?" *Professional Psychology: Research and Practice* 23, no. 2 (1992): 139–45.

Wanigarter, S. *Relapse Prevention for Addictive Behaviors: A Manual for Therapists*. Boston, MA: Blackwell Scientific, 1990.

"Who Knew? SOS for Surfaholics." *Seventeen*, July 1997, p. 52.

Wilson, P. H. *Principles and Practice of Relapse Prevention.* New York, NY: Guilford Press, 1993.

Winn, M. *The Plug-In Drug.* New York, NY: Viking Penguin, 1977.

Yearly, J. "The Use of Overeaters Anonymous in the Treatment of Eating Disorders." *Journal of Psychoactive Drugs* 19, no. 3 (1987):303–9.

Young, K. S. *The Addictive Reinforcers Underlying Internet Addiction Disorder.* Poster presented at the annual American Psychological Association conference on June 29, 1996, San Francisco, CA.

———. *Internet Addiction: The Emergence of a New Clinical Disorder.* Poster presented at the American Psychological Association conference on August 11, 1996, Toronto, Canada.

———. Pathological Internet Use: A case that breaks the stereotype. *Psychological Reports* 79 (1996):899–902.

———. *What Makes On-line Usage Stimulating: Potential Explanations for Pathological Internet Use.* Paper presented at the 105th meeting of the American Psychological Association, August 15, 1997, Chicago, IL.

———. The Relationship between Depression and Internet Addiction, *CyberPsychology and Behavior* 1 (1997):25–28.

# Index